THE BUSHWACKERS AUSTRALIAN SONG BOOK

Edited by
Jan Wositzky and Dobe Newton

Anne O'Donovan

Published by
Anne O'Donovan Pty Ltd
56 Claremont Street South Yarra Victoria 3141

First published in 1978
New edition 1981
Reprinted 1983
New edition 1988

Designed by Pam Brewster
Cover design by Lynn Twelftree

Music engraved by S. H. Newitt Melbourne
Set in Times by STL Industries Pty Ltd Melbourne
Printed by Globe Press Pty Ltd Melbourne
Distributed by Penguin Books Australia Ltd

ISBN 0 908476 31 0

FOREWORD

These are the folk songs of my country – the stories of a new and growing land that record a people's lives, hopes and disappointments in a way no history book has ever done. These songs tell of the guts and humour and perseverance of the convicts, pioneers and diggers who made this country what it is.

At an early age I came to love these songs but at the time hardly anyone in the music business, let alone the general public, was prepared to take this material seriously. Those days are over and it gives me great satisfaction to see the recognition now given to Australian traditional music.

I first met the Bushwackers several years ago and was delighted to find a group of young musicians who had discovered Australian folk music and had come to believe in it as passionately as I did. Now they have emerged as an exciting musical force, and are established as a popular recording and touring act both in Australia and in Europe.

They have put together a unique collection of material to convey their vision of the Australian character and attitudes, with vivid pictures just as relevant today as they were when first written and sung. May their Song Book help to spread an appreciation of Australia's rich folk tradition.

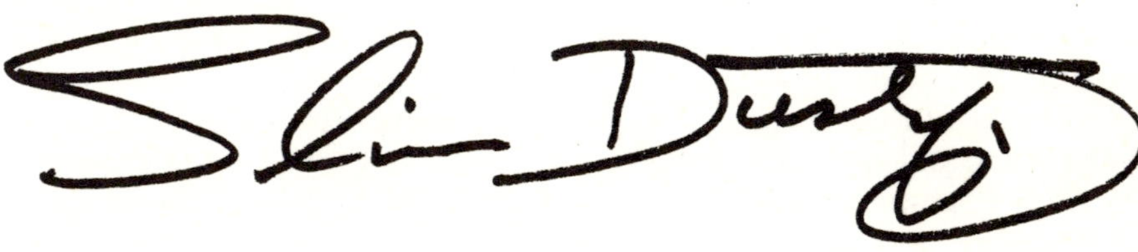

ACKNOWLEDGEMENTS

We are grateful firstly to all those who have researched and published before, and whose scholarship and interest in the Australian folk tradition has enabled so much material to survive. We would therefore like to thank Ron Edwards, Nancy Keesing and Douglas Stewart, John Manifold, John Meredith, Russel Ward, Bill Scott, Hugh Anderson, John Lahey, Bill Wannan and A. B. Paterson.

Secondly, and too numerous to mention individually, our thanks to the colleagues, wives and friends whose support allowed the book to grow, and whose enthusiasm enabled us to complete the project. For help with musical notation our thanks to Louis McManus, Mick Slocum, Chris Wendt and Geoff Boyd; and to David McCallum for his careful checking of the music. Our undying gratitude to Dave Harris and all the staff of the La Trobe Library, State Library of Victoria, who coped so graciously with all our requests. We are indebted also to the Mitchell Library in Sydney and the National Library in Canberra. Our thanks to Hiergraphics who designed the Band's logo and lastly thanks to Pam Brewster who designed the book.

Grateful acknowledgement for permission to reprint material in this book is made to the following: to Angus and Robertson, publishers of *The Collected Verse of A. B. Paterson*, and the Estate of A. B. Paterson for 'The Man from Ironbark', 'Clancy of the Overflow', 'A Bushman's Song' and the words of 'Waltzing Matilda'; to Slim Dusty and to Castle Music for permission to reproduce the song 'When the Rain Tumbles Down in July'; to Eric Bogle for his song 'And the Band Played Waltzing Matilda'.

For permission to reproduce illustrative material, we are grateful to the following: to Peter Lindsay of Sydney for the drawings by his father, the late Sir Lionel Lindsay; to Ure Smith for three Lionel Lindsay drawings from *The Romance of the Swag* by Henry Lawson; to Angus and Robertson for the Lionel Lindsay drawing from *On Our Selection* by Steele Rudd; to the copyright holder Jane Glad c/ Curtis Brown Australia Pty Ltd, Sydney and to the *Bulletin* for the Norman Lindsay drawings; to Angus and Robertson for the Percy Leason drawings; to Inglis Pty Ltd for the Billy Tea advertisement. For other material our thanks to the Mitchell Library, the La Trobe Library, State Library of Victoria, the National Library and the *Age*.

For permission to reproduce 'Lime-juice Tub' we are indebted to Image Music.

In a small number of cases we have been unable to trace the copyright holders and would appreciate any advice on omissions.

For these bush gems, thanks
to those who have sung
these songs and to those
who have listened.

CONTENTS

ON THE WALLABY

Now the tent poles are rotting, the camp fires are dead,
And the possums may gambol in trees overhead;
I am humping my bluey far out on the land,
And the prints of my bluchers sink deep in the sand:
I am out on the wallaby humping my drum,
And I came by the tracks where the sundowners come.

It is nor'-west and west o'er the ranges and far
To the plains where the cattle and sheep stations are,
With the sky for my roof and the grass for my bunk,
And a calico bag for my damper and junk;
And scarcely a comrade my memory reveals,
Save the spiritless dingo in tow of my heels.

But I think of the honest old light of my home
When the stars hang in clusters like lamps from the dome,
And I think of the hearth where the dark shadows fall,
When my camp fire is built on the widest of all;
But I'm following Fate, for I know she knows best,
I follow, she leads, and it's nor'-west by west.

When my tent is all torn and my blankets are damp,
And the rising flood waters flow fast by the camp,
When the cold water rises in jets from the floor,
I lie in my bunk and I list to the roar,
And I think how to-morrow my footsteps will lag
When I tramp 'neath the weight of a rain-sodden swag.

Though the way of the swagman is mostly up-hill,
There are joys to be found on the wallaby still.
When the day has gone by with its tramp or its toil,
And your camp fire you light, and your billy you boil,
There is comfort and peace in the bowl of your clay
Or the yarn of a mate who is tramping that way.

But beware of the town – there is poison for years
In the pleasure you find in the depths of long beers;
For the bushman gets bushed in the streets of a town,
Where he loses his friends when his cheque is knocked down;
He is right till his pockets are empty, and then –
He can hump his old bluey up country again.

Henry Lawson

JIM JONES AT BOTANY BAY

O listen for a moment lads,
And hear me tell my tale –
How o'er the sea from England's shore
I was condemned to sail.
The jury says, 'He's guilty, Sir'
And says the Judge, says he –
'For life, Jim Jones, I'm sending you
Across the stormy sea.'

'And take my tip before you ship
To join the iron gang,
Don't be too gay in Botany Bay
Or else you'll surely hang –
Or else you'll surely hang,' says he
'And after that Jim Jones,
It's high upon the gallows tree,
The crows they'll pick your bones.'

'You'll have no need for mischief there,
Remember what I say,
They'll flog the poaching hide off you
Out there at Botany Bay!'
The waves were high upon the sea,
The wind blew up in gales,
I would rather drown in misery
Than come to New South Wales.

The waves were high upon the sea
And the pirates came along,
But the soldiers on our convict ship
They were five hundred strong.
They opened fire and somehow drove
That pirate ship away,
I'd have rather joined the buccaneers,
Than come to Botany Bay.

For night and day the irons clang,
And like poor galley slaves,
We toil and toil, and when we die
Must fill dishonoured graves.
But by and by I'll break my chains
And to the bush I'll go,
And I'll join the bold bushrangers there –
Jack Donahoe and Co.

And late at night when everything
Is quiet in the town,
I'll kill the tyrants one and all,
I'll shoot the bastards down:
I'll give the law a little shock;
Remember what I say,
They'll yet regret they sent Jim Jones
In chains, to Botany Bay.

This is the oldest song we sing, and is in fact the earliest known Australian ballad. In terms of power and construction it stands head and shoulders above other songs of the period. As such we thought it deserved a more appropriate tune than the one it is usually sung to. The tune here was written by Mick Slocum.

MORETON BAY

One Sunday morning as I was walking,
By Brisbane waters I chanced to stray,
I heard a convict his fate bewailing
As on the sunny river bank he lay:
'I am a native of Erin's island
Transported now from my native shore,
They tore me from my aged parents
And from the maiden that I do adore.

'I've been a convict at Port Macquarie,
At Norfolk Island and Emu Plains,
At Castle Hill and cursed Toongabbie,
At all those settlements I've worked in chains;
But of all places of condemnation
And penal stations of New South Wales,
To Moreton Bay I have found no equal;
Excessive tyranny each day prevails.

'For three long years I was beastly treated
And heavy irons on my leg I wore;
My back with floggings was lacerated,
And often painted with my crimson gore.
And many a man from downright starvation
Lies mouldering now beneath the clay;
And Captain Logan he had us mangled
At the triangles of Moreton Bay.

'Like the Egyptians and ancient Hebrews
We were oppressed under Logan's yoke,
Till a native black lying there in ambush
Did deal our tyrant his mortal stroke.
My fellow prisoners, be exhilarated
That all such monsters such a death may find,
And when from bondage we are liberated,
Our former sufferings shall fade from mind.'

Frank McNamara was transported in the early 1820s, probably for forgery, and won a reputation throughout the colony for his wit and verses. The classical references in this fine song are typical of the man who took great and conscious pride in his nickname, 'The Poet'. Perhaps his best known work is a mammoth epic poem, 'A Convict's Tour of Hell' – a superb piece of sustained satire directed against Governor Darling and the whole penal system.

THE WILD COLONIAL BOY

There was a Wild Colonial Boy,
Jack Doolan was his name,
Of poor but honest parents
He was born in Castlemaine.
He was his father's only hope,
His mother's pride and joy
And dearly did his parents love
The Wild Colonial Boy.

Chorus:
So come away me hearties
We'll roam the mountains high,
Together we will plunder
And together we will die.
We'll scour along the valleys
And we'll gallop o'er the plains,
And scorn to live in slavery,
Bound down by iron chains.

At the age of sixteen years
He left his native home
And to Australia's sunny shores,
A bushranger did roam.
They put him in the iron gang
In the government employ,
But never an iron on earth could hold
The Wild Colonial Boy.

In sixty-one this daring youth
Commenced his wild career,
With a heart that knew no danger
And no foeman did he fear.
He stuck up the Beechworth mail coach
And robbed Judge MacEvoy
Who, trembling cold, gave up his gold
To the Wild Colonial Boy.

He bade the Judge good morning
And he told him to beware,
That he'd never rob a needy man
Or one who acted square,
But a Judge who'd rob a mother
Of her one and only joy
Sure, he must be a worse outlaw than
The Wild Colonial Boy.

One day as Jack was riding
The mountainside along,
A-listening to the little birds,
Their happy laughing song.
Three mounted troopers came along,
Kelly, Davis and Fitzroy
With a warrant for the capture of
The Wild Colonial Boy.

'Surrender now! Jack Doolan,
For you see it's three to one;
Surrender in the Queen's own name,
You are a highwayman.'
Jack drew a pistol from his belt
And waved it like a toy,
'I'll fight, but not surrender,' cried
The Wild Colonial Boy.

He fired at trooper Kelly
And brought him to the ground,
And in return from Davis
Received a mortal wound,
All shattered through the jaws he lay
Still firing at Fitzroy.
And that's the way they captured him,
The Wild Colonial Boy.

No historical evidence has as yet been advanced to prove the historical existence of Jack
Doolan, Duggan, Dolan etc. One plausible suggestion is that he was simply a character
based on the famous bushranger Jack Donahoe, who roamed NSW in the 1820s. Man or
myth – it hardly matters, as he has become the archetypal anti-establishment figure,
doing for bushranging what Robin Hood did for outlawry in England. We have
experienced the great popularity and knowledge of this song in Ireland and Britain.

But really, human life in this chaos of strangers of all nations, rushing frantically from every quarter of the earth to enrich themselves, is, as may be supposed, held wonderfully cheap. Who is likely to care for any one but himself? The number of unrecorded dead, who are found and put into a hasty grave, without anything frequently being known about them, is something frightful.

There have been instances of people entering a tent, and finding a solitary man in the last stage of illness, without a friend, or any means of help, where he has lain for days, or perhaps weeks, amid a busy multitude, all eager in their quest for gold, neither able to raise hand nor foot, nor cry for help, though there were people all around him. Others have been found dead in such a situation, with every sign of destruction about them, and not the slightest clue to who they were, or whence they came.

Out of hundreds of thousands of adventurers, English and foreign, how many have friends who would give almost their own lives to learn news of them! But they never will; for they either lie in those nameless graves or in these sixty and eighty feet deep shafts – now deserted, and their sides fallen in, burying their victims under many tons of clay.

W. Howitt, *Two Years in Victoria,* London, 1855

DENIS O'REILLY

When first I left old Ireland's shore,
The yarns that I was told,
Of how folks in Australia
Could dig up lumps of gold,
How gold dust lay in all the streets
And the miner's right was free.
Hurrah, says I, my loving friends
That's just the place for me.

Chorus:
With my swag all on my shoulder,
Black billy in my hand,
I'll travel the bushes of Australia,
Like a true-born native man.

And then we came to Melbourne town,
We all prepared to slip,
All bar the captain and the mate
All the crew abandoned ship,
And all the girls of Melbourne town
Threw up their hands with joy,
Sayin' one unto the other,
Here comes my Irish boy.

We made our way to Geelong town,
And north-west to Ballarat,
Where some of us grew mighty thin,
And some grew sleek and fat.
Some tried their luck at Bendigo
And some at Fiery Creek –
I made my fortune in a day,
And blue it in a week.

For many a long year I have travelled round
To each new field about.
I have made and spent full many a pound,
Till the alluvial petered out,
And now for any job of work
I am prepared to try
But now I've found the tucker track
I'll stay here till I die.

Within three years of gold being discovered, the population of Victoria quadrupled. Most of the new arrivals were the poor of Europe, come to strike it rich. While the miner's right was free, most of the unlucky managed to eke out a living, but the diggers reacted violently to government efforts to raise revenue by selling licences. Led by Peter Lalor, they eventually mounted an armed insurrection at the Eureka Stockade in 1854. The Republic they set up under the southern cross flag lasted some thirty-six hours, but Lalor went on to become a well-known political figure in the Ballarat area.

SHORES OF BOTANY BAY

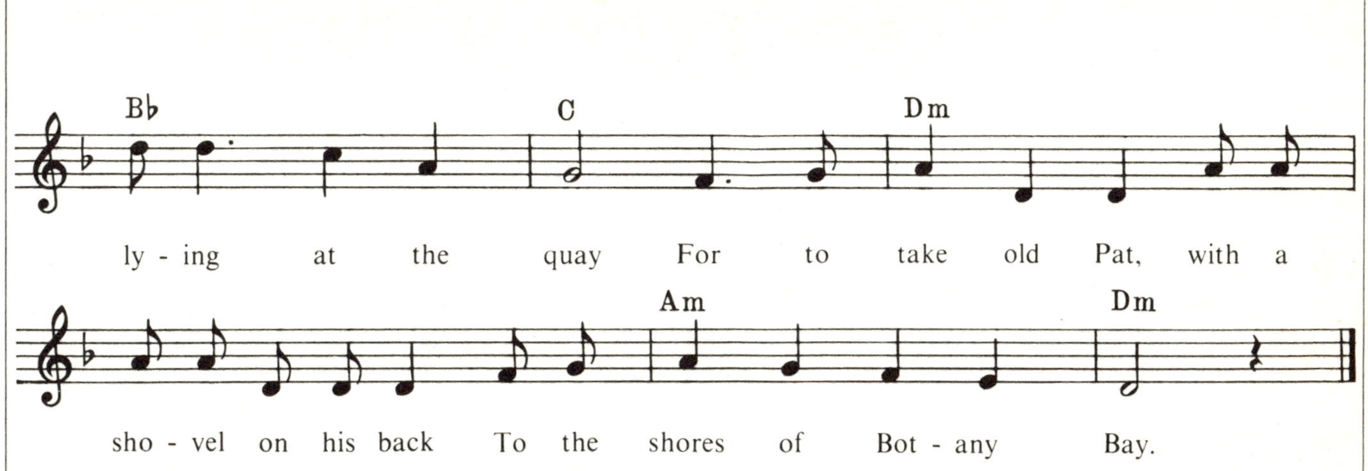

I'm on me way down to the quay
Where the big ship now doth lay,
To command a gang of navvies
I was ordered to engage,
And I thought I would stop in for a while
Before I sailed away
To take a trip, on an immigrant ship,
To the shores of Botany Bay.

Chorus:
Farewell to your bricks and mortar
Farewell to your dirty lime
Farewell to your gangway and your gang plank
And to hell with your overtime–
For the good ship Ragamuffin
She's lying at the quay
To take old Pat, with a shovel on his back
To the shores of Botany Bay.

The best years of our lives we spend
At working on the docks
Building mighty wharves and quays
Of earth and ballast rocks
Our pensions keep our lives secure,
But I'll not rue the day
When I take a trip, on an immigrant ship,
To the shores of Botany Bay.

The boss came out this morning
And he said 'Why Pat, hello,
If you do not mix the mortar quick
Be sure you'll have to go.'
Well of course he did insult me
And I demanded all me pay,
And I told him straight I was going to emigrate
To the shores of Botany Bay.

And when I reach Australia
I'll go and search for gold
There's plenty there for digging up
Or so I have been told.
Or maybe I'll go back to me trade,
Eight hundred bricks I'll lay
For an eight-hour shift and an eight bob pay
On the shores of Botany Bay.

BULLOCKY-O

I draw for Speckle's Mill, bullocky-O, bullocky-O,
It's many the log I drew, bullocky-O.
I draw cedar, beech and pine
And I never gets on the wine,
I'm king of the bullock drivers,
Don't you know, bullocky-O?
I'm king of the bullock drivers, don't you know?

There's Guinea and Anderson too, bullocky-O, bullocky-O,
It's many a log they drew, bullocky-O.
But I can give 'em a thousand feet,
Axe 'em square, and never cheat,
I'm king of the bullock drivers,
Don't you know, bullocky-O?
I'm king of the bullock drivers, don't you know?

There's Wapples too, he brags, bullocky-O, bullocky-O,
Of his forty raw-boned stags, bullocky-O.
But I tell you it's no slander,
When I say I raise their dander,
And they hear the crack of my whip
Bullocky-O, bullocky-O,
They hear the crack of my whip, bullocky-O.

'My first and longest-lasting experience of bullockies and their teams was in the Gippsland town of Bairnsdale (Vic.), where I lived as a youngster. I can still clearly recall the long lines of wagons, the bullocks leisurely moving, hauling their loads of wool, fruit and maize along the dusty roads to town. They seemed to disappear overnight, and in the late 1920s were completely replaced by mechanical transport. But in their heyday they were a sight not easily forgotten; and to my mind the teamsters were a superior brand of men, cast in the heroic mould.'

Bill Wannan, *Australasian Post* (May 12, 1960)

LIME-JUICE TUB

When shearing comes lay down your drums,
Step to the board, you brand new chums,
With a ra-dum-doo and a rub-a-dub-dub
We'll send you home in a lime-juice tub.

Since you have crossed the briny deep
You fancy you can shear a sheep,
With a ra-dum-doo and a rub-a-dub-dub
We'll send you home in a lime-juice tub.

Chorus:
Here we are in New South Wales
Shearing sheep as big as whales
With leather necks and daggy tails
and fleece as tough as rusty nails.

There's cockies' sons and brand new chums
Who fancy that they're all great guns.
They fancy they can shear the wool
The buggers can only tear and pull.

They tar the sheep till they're nearly black
Roll up, roll up, and get the sack
Once more we're away on the wallaby track
More to look for work out back.

And when they're out upon the road
From off their backs they throw their load
And at the sun they take a look
And reckon that it's time to press the cook.

They sleep in huts without any door
And camp upon the dirty floor,
With a pannikin of flour and a sheet of bark
To wallop up a damper in the dark.

You cockies, too, you never need fret
For I'm the man who's willing to bet
You're up to your eyes, heels first in debt
You're up to your eyes, your sons as well.

Although you live beyond your means,
Your daughters wear no crinolines
Nor are they covered by boots and shoes
They're wild in the bush with the kangaroos.

It's home, it's home I'd like to be,
Not humpin' me drum in this sheep country
Over a thousand miles I've come
To march along with a blanket drum.

But shearing's here, boys, give a cheer
Step to the board and grab your gear
With a ra-dum-doo and a rub-a-dub-dub
We'll send you home in a lime-juice tub.

FIVE MILES FROM GUNDAGAI

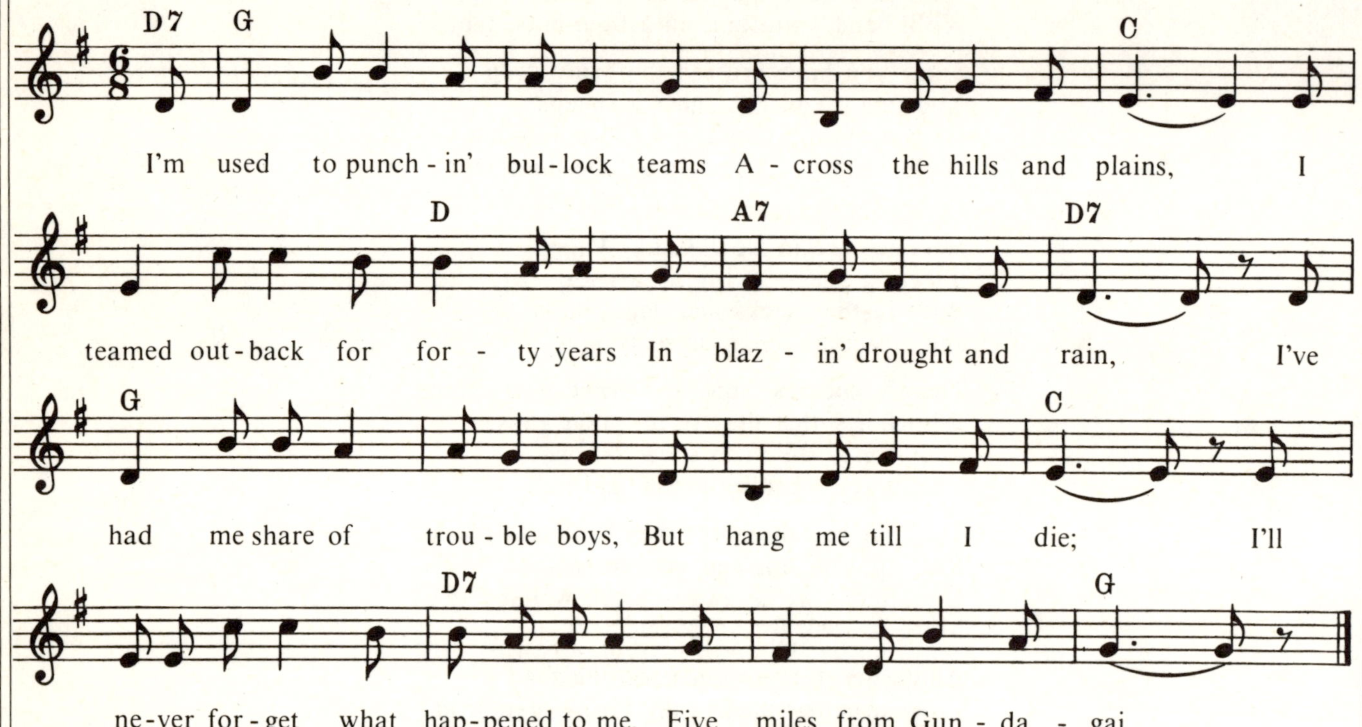

I'm used to punchin' bullock teams
Across the hills and plains,
I teamed outback for forty years
In blazin' drought and rain,
I've had me share of trouble boys,
But hang me till I die;
I'll never forget what happened to me,
Five miles from Gundagai.

It was raining hard, the team got bogged,
The axle snapped in two,
I'd lost me matches and me pipe,
Lord, what was I to do?
The rain came down, 'twas bitter cold,
And hungry too was I,
And the dog he shat in the tucker box,
Five miles from Gundagai.

Some blokes I know have lots of luck,
No matter where they fall.
But there was I, Lord love-a-duck!
No flamin' luck at all.
I couldn't make a pot of tea
Or keep me trousers dry,
And the dog,
He shat in me tucker box,
Five miles from Gundagai.

I can forgive the dark and cold,
I can forgive the rain.
I can forgive me flamin' team;
And go through it again.
I can forgive me rotten luck,
But hang me till I die,
I can't forgive that bloody dog,
Five miles from Gundagai.

All that now is past and gone,
I sold the team for meat.
And where I got the bullocks bogged,
Now there's an asphalt street.
The dog? Oh, well he took a bait,
And I reckoned that he'd died,
So I buried him in the tucker box,
Five miles from Gundagai.

Yes, all that now is past and gone,
And things are looking sweet,
Now I drive a big Mack truck,
In fact, I own a fleet.
I churn out lots of diesel fumes,
Turn people's faces sour,
And drive through bloody Gundagai,
At ninety miles an hour!

The last two verses were written by Tony Hunt. The spirit of the teamster lives on in the
truckies. He finally has his revenge on Gundagai.

MARANOA DROVERS

Oh, the night is dark and stormy
And the sky is clouded o'er,
Our horses we will mount and ride away,
To watch the squatter's cattle
Through the darkness of the night
And we'll keep them on the camp till break of day.

Chorus:
For we're going, going, going
To Gunnedah so far
Soon we'll be in sunny New South Wales,
And we'll bid farewell to Queensland
With its swampy coolibah
Happy drovers from the sandy Maranoa.

With our campfires burning bright
Through the darkness of the night,
And the cattle camping quiet, well, I'm sure
That I wish for two o'clock
When I call the other watch,
This is droving on the sandy Maranoa.

With our beds made on the ground
We are sleeping oh so sound,
We're wakened by the thunder's distant roar
And the lightning's vivid flash,
Followed by an awful crash
Rough on drovers from the sandy Maranoa.

We are up at break of day,
And we'll soon be on our way,
We always have to go ten miles or more,
But it don't do to loaf about,
Or the squatter will come out
He's rough on drovers from the sandy Maranoa.

We'll soon be on the Moonie
And we'll cross the Barwon too,
Then out upon the rolling plains once more,
And we'll shout 'Hurrah', for Queensland
And its swampy coolibah,
And the cattle that come off the Maranoa.

THE SHEARER'S NIGHTMARE

Old Bill the shearer had been phoned to catch the train next day –
He had a job at Mungindi, an early start for May,
So he packed his port and rolled his swag and hurried off to bed,
But sleep he couldn't steal a wink to soothe his aching head.

He heard the missus snoring hard, he heard the ticking clock,
He heard the midnight train blow in, he heard the crowin' cock.
At last Bill in a stupor lay, a-dreaming now was he
Of sheep, and pens, and belly wool he shore in number three.

He grabbed the missus in his sleep and shore her like a ewe.
The first performance soon was done as up the neck he flew,
And then he turned to long-blow her, down the whipping side he tore
With his mighty knee upon her and his grip around her jaw.

And then he rolled her over, like a demon now he shore
She dare not kick or struggle, she had seen him shear before.
He was leading Jack the ringer, he was matching Mick the Brute
When he called for 'tar' and he dumped her like a hogget down the chute.

Then he reached to stop the shear machine, all excited and out of gear
And the electric light was shining, and all was bright and clear
He gazed now out the window, half awakened from his sleep
And down there on the footpath lay his missus in a heap.

'Gawd Blimey, I've had nightmares, after boozin' up a treat
And I walked without no trousers to the pub across the street
But this one here takes lickin' and it's one I'll have to keep
I dare not tell the cobbers I shore the missus in me sleep!'

Anon.

POOR NED KELLY

When Ned was a lad, sixteen years old,
He received a horse that his best mate stole.
And the judge just to give him time to think.
Gave him three months hard in the local clink.

Chorus:
Poor Ned Kelly,
It's easier to do today,
Poor Ned Kelly,
They don't even have to run away.

Ned got out, he went straight for a while,
He worked very hard but he couldn't make a pile.
The coppers used to bully his poor old mum,
So he stole their horses and away he run.

Now Ned, and his gang they ran fast and free,
They stuck up the town of Jerilderie.
They took all the local troopers and locked 'em away,
Then they entertained the people for the rest of the day.

It was at Glenrowan that they took old Ned
He wore a suit of armour and they couldn't shoot him dead.
So they took him down to Melbourne, and wouldn't go him bail,
And they hung him from a rafter in the Russell Street gaol.

'Smiling' Billy Blinkhorn

STRINGYBARK CREEK

A sergeant and three constables rode out from Mansfield Town
Near the end of last October for to hunt the Kellys down;
They headed for the Wombat Hills and thought it quite a lark
To be camped along the borders of a creek called Stringybark.

When Scanlon and the sergeant rode away to search the scrub
Leaving MacIntyre and Lonigan in camp to cook the grub,
Ned Kelly and his comrades came to take a nearer look,
For being short of flour they wished to interview the cook.

Both troopers at a stump alone they were well pleased to see
Watching as the billy boiled to make their pints of tea;
They joked and chatted gaily, never thinking of alarm
Till they heard the dreaded cry behind, 'Bail up, throw down your arms!'

The traps they started wildly and Mac then firmly stood
While Lonigan made tracks to gain the cover of the wood,
But brave Kelly muttered sadly as he loaded up his gun,
'Oh, what a flamin' pity that the bastard tried to run.'

'Twas later in the afternoon the sergeant and his mate
Came riding blithely through the bush to meet a cruel fate.
'The Kellys have the drop on you!' cried MacIntyre aloud,
But the troopers took it as a joke and sat their horses proud.

Then trooper Scanlon made a move his rifle to unsling,
But to his heart a bullet sped and death was in its sting;
Then Kennedy leapt from his mount and ran for cover near,
And fought, a game man to the last, for all that life held dear.

The sergeant's horse raced from the camp alike from friend and foe,
And MacIntyre, his life at stake, sprang to the saddle-bow
And galloped far into the night, a haunted, harassed soul,
Then like a hunted bandicoot hid in a wombat hole.

At dawn of day he hastened forth and made for Mansfield town
To break the news that made men vow to shoot the Kellys down.
So from that hour the Kelly gang was hunted far and wide,
Like outlaw dingoes in the wild until the day they died.

As the last verse of the song points out, from that day in October 1878, time began to run
out for the Kellys. It was for the murder of Sergeant Kennedy that Ned was tried and
convicted in November 1880. Kelly stalked the already wounded policeman into the
Stringybark forest and shot him dead. Opinion is still fiercely divided as to whether it was
an act of mercy (as supporters claim), or one of cold blooded murder, as the prosecution
claimed at the trial.

NED KELLY'S FAREWELL TO GLENROWAN

The Kelly Gang were bushrangers with a price on their heads when, on Sunday afternoon, June 27 1880, they were gathered at the Glenrowan Inn with sixty hostages – many of whom were Kelly supporters.

The gang were confident and in good humour. There was plenty of liquor and Ned made speeches about the injustices done to his family by the Victorian Police.

One of the hostages had a concertina, and the bushrangers danced jigs and reels, stepping it out with the locals. The floorboards creaked as they flung themselves into a Heel and Toe Polka, the Varsovienna and the Walls of Limerick – a dance from 'home'. The concertina, squeezed by dirty, cracked hands, sprang back and forth spitting notes at those waiting outside in the yard and down by the railway line.

The festivities continued until shortly after three the following morning. The last wild dance, 'Ned Kelly's Farewell to Glenrowan', was halted when it was discovered that a trainload of armed police had surrounded the inn.

The hostages took cover while Ned, Dan, Steve Hart and Joe Byrne prepared to fight their last battle together.

So, ladies and gentlemen, take your partners for 'Ned Kelly's Farewell to Glenrowan'.

Six couples form a set, men and women in lines facing each other. The lines should be about eight feet apart. The couple nearest the band is called the 'top' couple, and to begin –

1 The top lady and the bottom man take four steps forward diagonally across the set to arrive in the centre (Fig. A). They link right arms, turn once and return with four steps to their places. This movement is repeated by the top man and bottom lady. So far we have had 8 bars of music.

2 Same again, except this time the turn is on the left arm (8 bars).

3 Then the turn is done with both hands outstretched, and back to your place (8 bars).

4 Same two couples doci-do. That is, with arms folded across the chest you meet in the centre of the set and circle one another back to back (8 bars).

5 Meet in the middle and bow (8 bars).

6 Move straight across the set to your partner and swing. This is best done if both place their right hands on their partner's left hip, joining left hands underneath. (The left arm passes outside and beneath the hand on your hip and grips the hand.) You can now swing like old Ned hisself and lean back for extra speed (8 bars).

7 Line up in your original positions and all turn to face the top of the set. In single file follow the respective top man and top woman as they turn outwards and skip down the outside of the set (Fig. B). When they meet at the bottom, the top couple joins hands facing each other, standing as far apart as possible to form an arch. The following couples take their partner's hand and proceed under this arch (Fig. C). The first couple under leads the rest up to the top, thus becoming the new top couple. The old top couple are now the bottom couple and the dance begins again (16 bars).

This dance can be performed to any Irish jig of thirty-two bars (played through twice to complete the movements described above).

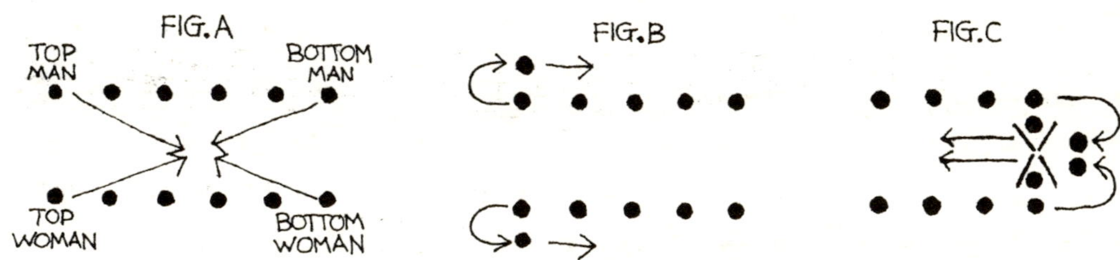

WOOLLOOMOOLOO LAIR

On the day that I was born
It was a cold and a frosty morn,
In the famous suburb known as Woolloomooloo,
It was down in Riley Street
My folks first heard me bleat
'Cause at the time I'd nothing else to do.
Now me mother died of fright
When she saw me in the light,
And me father thought he'd send me to the zoo
But I owe a lot to him,
'Cause he taught me how to swim
When he heaved me off the pier at Woolloomooloo.

Chorus:
Oh me name it is McCarty,
And I'm a rorty party
I'm rough and tough as an old man kangaroo
Some people say I'm crazy,
I don't work because I'm lazy
And I tag along in the boozin' throng, the push from Woolloomooloo.

And when I was just a lad
I went straight'way to the bad
A larrikin so hard, you'd strike me blue
But the government was kind
And they didn't seem to mind
In Darlinghurst I spent a night or two.
Now the judge gave me a stare
And he said, 'You're a lair,'
They heaved me into Darlinghurst gaol – you understand,
They gave me clothes, they cut me hair
I didn't seem to care
And every night you'd find me in the van.

And I spent some years in gaol,
Till I began to quail
I resolved to live upon a different lay
And enlisted in the ranks
Of the Salvation Army 'cranks'
You can bet I made the bloody business pay!
Hallelujah! I'm a lout,
I knows me way about
I kids the mugs that I'm converted too
All the lasses there I mash,
And I'm never short of cash
'Cause I beats the drum all over Woolloomooloo.

Here is one of the rare city songs. The 1890s saw Sydney's inner suburbs alive with gangs
of larrikins, of frustrated bearing and ill intent. Most often living within the shadow of
violence, they were flash dressers from the poorer cramped areas. They have been
paralleled in recent times by skinheads, sharpies, droogs and bodgies. However, our man
McCarty from the 'push' approaches the problems of inner suburban living with a good
deal more wit and invention than his modern-day counterparts.

THE NEW CHUM

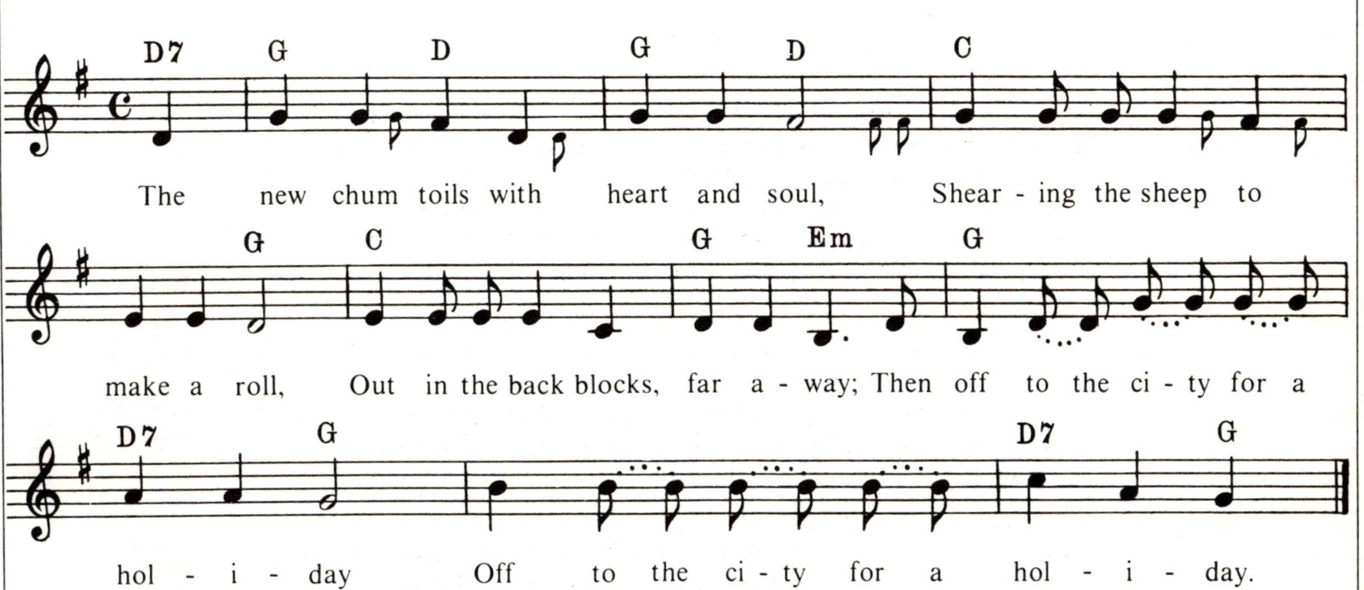

The new chum toils with heart and soul,
Shearing the sheep to make a roll,
Out in the back blocks, far away;
Then off to the city for a holiday –
Off to the city for a holiday.

Refrain:
Last line of every verse

And down in the city he looks a swell,
And he catches a taxi to the Kent Hotel,
The barmaid says, 'My you look ill!
It must have been rough tucker, Bill.'

And down in the city he looks a goat,
In his Oxford bags and Seymour coat.
He spends his money like a fool of course;
That he worked for like a flamin' horse.

And he shouts for all hands round the place,
And it's off to Randwick for the big horse race.
He dopes himself on back-ache pills,
He talks high tallies and tucker bills.

Now his money's gone, he's stiff and sore,
And the barmaid isn't so kind no more.
His erstwhile friends don't give a hoot,
So it's back to the bush, per what? – the boot!

And his money's gone and he can't get booze,
And his socks are showing through his snake-skin shoes.
He's lost his beautiful Seymour coat;
He's got no money – oh, what a goat.

So he stands on the corner, cadging fags,
With his shirt tails showing through his Oxford bags;
And he camps in the bend, in the wind and rain
And waits for the shearing to start again.

So all you fellas with a cheque to spend,
Don't go down to the city where you've got no friends,
Go to the nearest wayside shack –
It's not so far, when you've got to walk back!

Making a fool of the naive bushman has long been considered an amusing and reasonable 'sport' by Australian townsfolk. The bushmen very often did not appreciate the 'joke', and we can be certain that any who suffered as this song suggests would not pass up their opportunity for a bit of fun when the roles were reversed.

THE MAN FROM IRONBARK

It was the man from Ironbark who struck the Sydney town,
He wandered over street and park, he wandered up and down.
He loitered here, he loitered there, till he was like to drop,
Until at last in sheer despair he sought a barber's shop.
"Ere! shave my beard and whiskers off, I'll be a man of mark,
I'll go and do the Sydney toff up home in Ironbark.'

The barber man was small and flash, as barbers mostly are,
He wore a strike-your-fancy sash, he smoked a huge cigar:
He was a humorist of note and keen at repartee,
He laid the odds and kept a 'tote', whatever that may be.
And when he saw our friend arrive, he whispered 'Here's a lark!
Just watch me catch him all alive this man from Ironbark.'

There were some gilded youths that sat along the barber's wall,
Their eyes were dull, their heads were flat, they had no brains at all;
To them the barber passed the wink, his dexter eyelid shut,
'I'll make this bloomin' yokel think his bloomin' throat is cut.'
And as he soaped and rubbed it in he made a rude remark:
'I s'pose the flats is pretty green up there in Ironbark.'

A grunt was all reply he got; he shaved the bushman's chin,
Then made the water boiling hot and dipped the razor in.
He raised his hand, his brow grew black, he paused a while to gloat,
Then slashed the red-hot razor-back across his victim's throat;
Upon the newly-shaven chin it made a livid mark –
No doubt it fairly took him in – the man from Ironbark.

He fetched a wild up-country yell might wake the dead to hear,
And though his throat, he knew full well, was cut from ear to ear,
He struggled gamely to his feet, and faced the murderous foe.
'You've done for me! you dog, I'm beat! one hit before I go!
I only wish I had a knife, you blessed murdering shark!
But you'll remember all your life the man from Ironbark.'

He lifted up his hairy paw, with one tremendous clout
He landed on the barber's jaw, and knocked the barber out.
He set to work with tooth and nail, he made the place a wreck;
He grabbed the nearest gilded youth, and tried to break his neck.
And all the while his throat he held to save his vital spark,
And 'Murder! Bloody Murder!' yelled the man from Ironbark.

A peeler man who heard the din came in to see the show;
He tried to run the bushman in, but he refused to go.
And when at last the barber spoke, and said "Twas all in fun –
'Twas just a harmless little joke, a trifle overdone.'
'A joke!' he cried, 'By George, that's fine; a lively sort of lark;
I'd like to catch that murdering swine some night in Ironbark.'

And now while round the shearing-floor the listening shearers gape,
He tells the story o'er and o'er, and brags of his escape.
'Them barber chaps what keeps a tote, by George, I've had enough,
One tried to cut my bloomin' throat, but thank the Lord it's tough.'
And whether he's believed or no, there's one thing to remark,
That flowing beards are all the go way up in Ironbark.

A. B. ('Banjo') Paterson

THE 'MATILDA WALTZERS' UNION

In 1877 the 'professional' swagmen – those who were swagmen by choice – formed their own 'union'. The inaugural meeting was held on the Lachlan River near Forbes in NSW and a collection of 'frowsy deadbeats, loony hatters and aggressive cadgers' got together to vote for office bearers and draw up regulations:

1. No member to be over 100 years old.
2. Each member to pay one pannikin of flour entrance fee. Members who don't care about paying will be admitted free.
3. No member to carry swags weighing over 10 lb.
4. Each member to possess three complete sets of tucker-bags, each set to consist of nine bags.
5. No member to pass any station, farm, boundary-rider's hut, camp, or private house without 'tapping' and obtaining rations and hand-outs.
6. No member to allow himself to be bitten by a sheep. If a sheep bites a member he must immediately turn it into mutton.
7. Members who defame a 'good' cook or pay a fine when run in shall be expelled from the Union.
8. No member is allowed to hum baking powder, tea, flour, sugar, or tobacco from a fellow-unionist.
9. Non-smoking members must 'whisper' for tobacco on every possible occasion, the same as other smokers.
10. At general or branch meetings non-smokers must ante up their whispered tobacco nuggets to be distributed amongst the officers of the Union.
11. Any member found without having at least two sets of bags filled with tucker will be fined.
12. No member to own more than one creek, river, or billabong bend. To sell bends for old boots or 'sinkers' is prohibited.
13. No member to look for or accept work of any description. Members found working will be at once expelled.
14. No member to walk more than five miles per day if rations can be hummed.
15. No member to tramp on Sundays at any price.

A further effort to give swagmen some kind of official status was a strange publication that appeared in 1900 entitled 'The Swag: The Unofficial Flute of the Sundowners and Other Colonial Vagrants; with which is enfurcated the Bush Marconi and the Whaler's Telegraph'.

The publication was aimed at the Governor-General, Lord Hopetoun, in the hope that he would obtain a better deal for the wanderers of the bush.

Amongst other things, the author reckoned that swaggies and their ilk, being true blue Aussies, should be represented at the functions celebrating the inauguration of the Commonwealth!

WALTZING MATILDA

Once a jolly swagman camped by a billabong,
Under the shade of a coolibah tree,
And he sang as he sat and watched his billy boiling,
Who'll come a-Waltzing Matilda with me?

Chorus:
Waltzing Matilda, Matilda my darling,
Who'll come a-waltzing Matilda with me,
Waltzing Matilda and leading a water bag
Who'll come a-waltzing Matilda with me?

Along came a jumbuck and he drank from the billabong,
Down jumped the swagman and he grabbed him with glee,
And he sang as he shoved that jumbuck in his tucker bag,
You'll come a-waltzing Matilda with me.

Chorus:
Waltzing Matilda, Matilda my darling,
Who'll come a-waltzing Matilda with me,
Waltzing Matilda and leading a water bag
You'll come a-waltzing Matilda with me.

Down came the squatter mounted on his thoroughbred;
Down came the troopers, one, two, three,
Whose is the jumbuck you've got in your tucker bag?
You'll come a-waltzing Matilda with me.

Chorus:
Waltzing Matilda, Matilda my darling,
Who'll come a-waltzing Matilda with me,
Waltzing Matilda and leading a water bag
You'll come a-waltzing Matilda with me.

Well up jumped the swagman and he leapt into the billabong,
He drowned himself by the coolibah tree,
And his ghost may be heard as you pass by the billabong,
Who'll come a-waltzing Matilda with me?

Chorus:
Waltzing Matilda, Matilda my darling,
Who'll come a-waltzing Matilda with me,
Waltzing Matilda and leading a water bag
Who'll come a-waltzing Matilda with me?

Adapted from A. B. ('Banjo') Paterson

'Banjo' Paterson first heard the term in 1895, whilst on a visit to Dagworth station, Central Queensland. On the road to Winton the buggy passed a nomad with a cylindrical blanket roll on his back. Robert Macpherson, his host, explained that he called this 'waltzing Matilda'. The term has an obvious affinity with the German *waltz-bruder* meaning 'rolling brother'.

Legend has it that by the time the party reached Winton the story was penned and put to a tune that evening. So the full-blown lifestyle of the Australian itinerant was classically captured in just two words, and the age-old cry of the poor, struggling along beside the landed, was given a powerful Australian voice. The tune here is the original, and not the 'popular' one which arrived later and was an old recruiting ballad from the time of the Duke of Marlborough.

AND THE BAND PLAYED WALTZING MATILDA

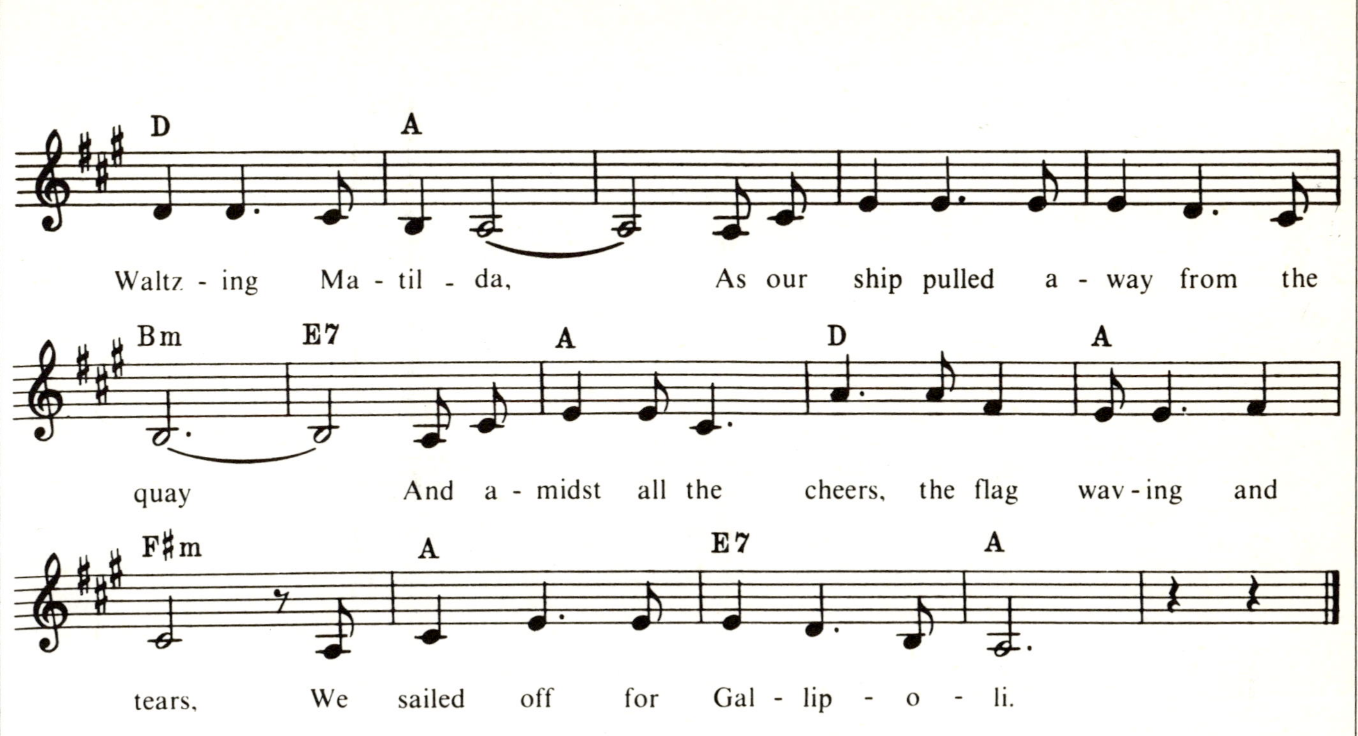

When I was a young man I carried a pack
And I lived the free life of a rover,
From the Murray's green banks to the dusty outback,
I waltzed my matilda all over.
Then in 1915, the country said, 'Son,
There's no time for rovin', there's work to be done,'
And they gave me a tin hat, and gave me a gun,
And they sent me away to the war.
And the band played Waltzing Matilda,
As our ship pulled away from the quay
And amidst all the cheers, the flag-waving and tears
We sailed off for Gallipoli.

How well I remember that terrible day
When our blood stained the sand and the water,
And how in that hell that they called Suvla Bay,
We were butchered like lambs at the slaughter.
Johnny Turk he was waiting, he'd primed himself well,
He showered us with bullets, and rained us with shell,
And in ten minutes flat, he'd blown us to hell:
Nearly blew us right back to Australia.
And the band played Waltzing Matilda,
As we stopped to bury the slain.
We buried ours and the Turks buried theirs,
Then we started all over again.

They collected the crippled, the wounded and maimed
And they shipped us back home to Australia,
The armless, the legless, the blind and insane,
All the brave wounded heroes of Suvla.
And when our ship pulled into Circular Quay,
And I looked at the place where my legs used to be,
I thanked Christ there was nobody waiting for me –
To grieve, and to mourn and to pity.
And the band played Waltzing Matilda
As they carried us down the gangway,
But nobody cheered, they just stood there and stared –
And then turned their faces away.

So now every April I sit on my porch,
And I watch the parade pass before me,
And I see my old comrades how proudly they march,
Reliving old dreams and past glories.
But the old men march slowly their bones stiff and sore –
Tired old men from a tired old war,
And the young people ask what are they marching for,
And I ask myself the same question.
But the band played Waltzing Matilda
And the old men they answer the call,
But year by year those old men disappear
Soon no one will march there at all.

Eric Bogle

As a part of Allied strategy, it was decided, early in 1915 to attack Turkey through the Dardanelles so providing a safe sea-link with Russia. After an abortive attempt by the Royal Navy, it became a military operation against a powerful and forewarned enemy occupying almost impregnable positions atop rugged cliffs. On April 25, the Australians landed at Suvla Bay and after a day of heroic and bloody fighting established a precarious foothold at what became known as Anzac Cove. During the next few months, weeks of stalemate were interspersed with days of bitter fighting. In this futile exercise, which ended with evacuation in January 1916, the Australian casualties were 9000 dead and 20 000 wounded. A national holiday was declared to honour the dead and celebrate the outstanding gallantry of the 'Diggers'.

Eric Bogle arrived from Scotland only a few years ago, and had only been here for two years when he wrote this song. It is testimony to a rare talent that a 'stranger' could have captured all the subtleties of Anzac Day as we know it. A beautiful and evocative piece of writing it will certainly live on as one of the greatest Australian compositions. The song has also been very popular in Canada and Ireland (No. 1 on the charts) where it is sung with a passion against the futility of war.

This version has developed from the band's stage performance, and varies slightly from Eric Bogle's original words and music.

THE ROMANCE OF THE SWAG

The Australian swag fashion is the easiest way in the world of carrying a load. I ought to know something about carrying loads ... I've carried a portmanteau on the hot dusty roads in green old Jackeroo days. Ask any actor who's been stranded and had to count railway sleepers from one town to another! He'll tell you what sort of an awkward load a portmanteau is, especially if there's a broken-hearted man underneath it. I've tried knapsack fashion – one of the least healthy and most likely to give a man sores; I've carried my belongings in a three-bushel sack slung over my shoulder – blankets, tucker, spare boots and poetry all lumped together. I tried carrying a load on my head, and got a crick in my neck and spine for days. I've carried a load on my mind that should have been shared by editors and publishers. I've helped hump luggage and furniture up to, and down from, a top flat in London. And I've carried swag for months out-back in Australia – and it was life, in spite of its 'squalidness' and meanness and wretchedness and hardship, and in spite of the fact that the world would have regarded us as 'tramps' – and a free life amongst *men* from all the world!

The Australian swag was born of Australia and no other land – of the Great Lone Land of magnificent distances and bright heat; the land of Self-reliance, and Never-give-in, and Help-your-mate. The grave of many of the world's tragedies and comedies – royal and otherwise. The land where a man out of employment might shoulder his swag in Adelaide and take the track, and years later walk into a hut on the Gulf, or never be heard of any more, or a body be found in the Bush and buried by the mounted police, or never found and never buried – what does it matter?

The land I love above all others – not because it was kind to me, but because I was born on Australian soil, and because of the foreign father who died at his work in the ranks of Australian pioneers, and because of many things. Australia! my country! her very name is music to me. God bless Australia! for the sake of the great hearts of the heart of her! ...

In the old digging days the knapsack, or straps-across-the-chest fashion, was tried, but the load pressed on a man's chest and impeded his breathing, and a man needs to have his bellows free on long tracks in hot, stirless weather. Then the 'horse-collar', or rolled military overcoat style – swag over one shoulder and under the other arm – was tried, but it was found to be too hot for the Australian climate, and was discarded along with Wellington boots and leggings. Until recently, Australian city artists and editors – who knew as much about the Bush as Downing Street knows about the British colonies in general – seemed to think the horse-collar swag was still in existence; and some artists gave the swagman a stick, as if he were a tramp of civilisation with an eye on the backyard and a fear of the dog. English artists, by the way, seem firmly convinced that the Australian bushman is born in Wellington boots with a polish on 'em you could shave yourself by.

The swag is usually composed of a tent 'fly' or strip of calico (a cover for the swag and a shelter in bad weather – in New Zealand it is oilcloth or waterproof twill), a couple of blankets, blue by custom and preference, as that colour shows the dirt less than any other (hence the name 'bluey' for swag), and the core is composed of spare clothing and small personal effects. To make or 'roll up' your swag: lay the fly or strip of calico on the ground, blueys on top of it; across one end, with eighteen inches or so to spare, lay your spare trousers, shirt, etc., folded, light boots tied together by the laces toe to heel, books, bundle of old letters, portraits, or whatever little knick-knacks you have or care to carry, bag of needles, thread, pen and ink, spare patches for your pants, bootlaces, etc., lay or arrange the pile so that it will roll evenly with the swag (some pack the lot in an old pillowslip or canvas bag), take a fold over of blanket and calico the whole length on each side, so as to reduce the width of the swag to, say, three feet, throw the spare end, with an inward fold, over the little pile of belongings, and then roll the whole to the other end, using your knees and judgment to make the swag tight, compact and artistic; when within eighteen inches of the loose end take an inward fold in that, and bring it up against the body of the swag. There is a strong suggestion of a roley-poley in a rag about the business, only the ends of the swag are folded in, in rings, and not tied. Fasten the swag with three or four straps, according to judgment and the supply of straps. To the top strap, for the swag is carried (and eased down in shanty bars and against walls or verandah-posts when not on the track) in a more or less vertical position – to the top strap, and lowest, or lowest but one, fasten the ends of the shoulder strap (usually a towel is preferred as being softer to the shoulder), your coat being carried outside the swag at the back, under the straps. To the top strap fasten the string of the nose-bag, a calico bag about the size of a pillowslip, containing the tea, sugar and flour bags, bread, meat, baking powder, salt, etc., and brought, when the swag is carried from the left shoulder, over the right on to the chest, and so balancing the swag behind. But a swagman can throw a heavy swag in a nearly vertical position against his spine, slung from one shoulder only and without any balance, and carry it as easily as you might wear your overcoat. Some Bushmen arrange their belongings so neatly and conveniently, with swag straps in a sort of harness, that they can roll up the swag in about a minute, and unbuckle it and throw it out as easily as a roll of wall-paper, and there's the bed ready on the ground with the wardrobe for a pillow. The swag is always used for a seat on the track; it is a soft seat, so trousers last a long time. And, the dust being mostly soft and silky on the long tracks out-back, boots last marvellously. Fifteen miles a day is the average with the swag, but you must travel according to the water: if the next bore or tank is five miles on, and the next twenty beyond, you camp at the five-mile water to-night and do the twenty next day. But if it's thirty miles you have to do it. Travelling with the swag in Australia is variously and picturesquely described as 'humping bluey', 'walking Matilda', 'humping Matilda', 'humping your drum', 'being on the wallaby', 'jabbing trotters' and 'tea and sugar burglaring', but most travelling shearers now call themselves trav'lers, and say simply 'on the track', or 'carrying swag'.

And there you have the Australian swag.

From *The Romance of the Swag* by Henry Lawson

JOG ALONG TILL SHEARING

The truth is in my song so clear
Without a word of gammon:
The swagman travels all the year
Waiting for the lambin'.
When his dirty work is done,
To the nearest shanty steering,
They meet a friend, their money spend,
Then jog along till shearing.

Chorus:
Home, sweet home,
That is what they left it for,
Their home, sweet home.

Now when the shearing season comes,
They hear the price that's going;
New arrivals meet old chums,
Then they start their blowing.
They say that they can shear each day
Their hundred pretty handy,
But eighty sheep is bloody hard
When the wool is close and sandy.

Now when the sheds have all cut out
They get their bit of paper,
To the nearest pub they run
To cut a dash and caper.
They call for liquor plenty
And are happy while they're drinking,
But where they'll go when their money's done,
It's little they'll be thinking.

Sick and sore next morning
They are when they awaken.
To have a drink of course they must
To keep their nerves from shaking,
They call for one, and then for two
In a way that's rather funny,
Till the landlord says, 'Now, this won't do,
You men have got no money.'

They're leaning on verandah posts
And loafing on the sofas,
For to finish off their spree,
They're ordered off as loafers.
They've got no friends, their money's gone
And at their disappearing
They give three cheers for the river bend
And jog along till shearing.

THE BACKBLOCK SHEARER

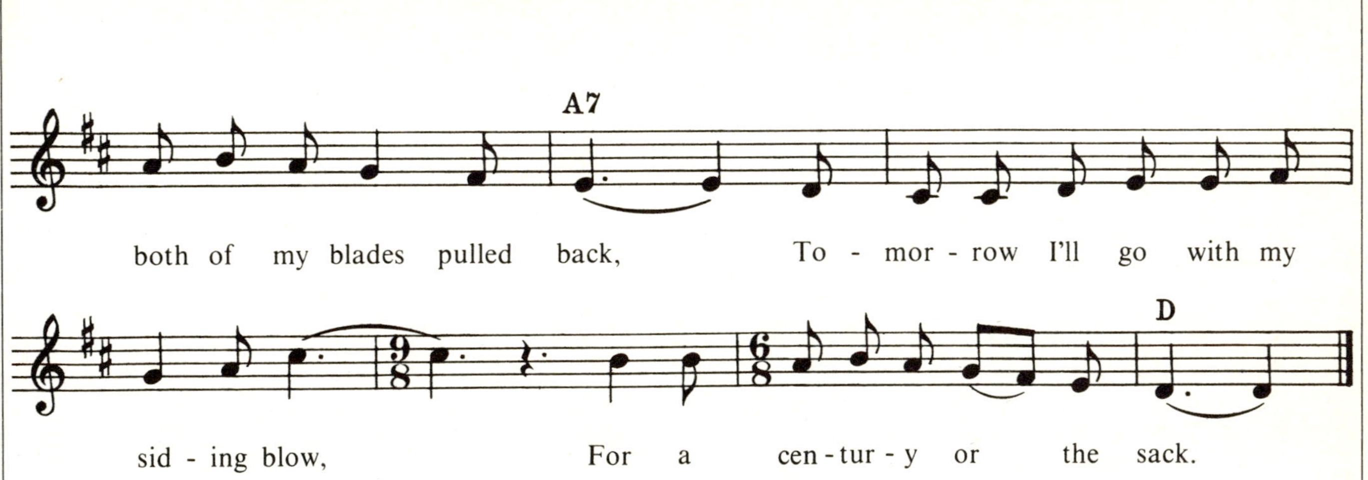

I'm only a backblock shearer boys,
As easily can be seen,
I've shore in most of the famous sheds
On the plains of the Riverine.
I've shore in most of the famous sheds
And seen the big tallies done,
But somehow or other I don't know why
I never became a gun.

Chorus:
Hurrah my boys, my blades are set,
And I feel both fit and well.
Tomorrow you'll find me at my pen,
When the gaffer rings the bell.
With Haydon's patent thumb-guards fixed,
And both of my blades pulled back.
Tomorrow I'll go with my siding blow,
For a century or the sack.

I've opened up the windpipe straight,
I've opened behind the ear,
I've shore in every possible style
In which a man can shear.
I've studied all the cuts and drives
Of famous men I've met,
But I've never succeeded in plastering up
Those three little figures yet.

The boss walked down the board this morning,
I saw him stare at me,
I'd mastered Moran's great shoulder cut,
As he could plainly see.
But I've another surprise for him
That will give his nerves a shock,
For tomorrow I'll show him that I have mastered
Pierce's rang-tang block.

And when I succeed, as I hope to do,
Then I intend to shear,
At the Wagga demonstration,
That's held there every year.
It's there I'll lower the colours, my boys,
The colours of Mitchell and Co.
And instead of Deeming you will hear
Of Widgeegoweera Joe.

The Deeming referred to in this song was for a time a very famous man indeed. He was variously described by the press as 'The Criminal of the Century', 'Jack the Ripper of the Southern Seas' and 'The Modern Bluebeard'. He was hanged in 1892 for the murder of his first wife and four children in London, and his second wife in Melbourne.

THE SPRINGTIME IT BRINGS ON THE SHEARING

The springtime it brings on the shearing,
And it's then you will see them in droves,
To the west-country stations all steering,
A-seeking a job off the coves.

Chorus:
With my raggedy old swag on my shoulder
And a billy quart-pot in my hand,
I tell you we'll 'stonish the new chums,
When they see how we travel the land.

From Boonabri up to the border,
Then it's over to Bourke; there and back.
On the hills and the plains you will see them,
The men on the Wallaby Track.

And after the shearing is over
And the wool season's all at an end,
It is then you will see the flash shearers
Making johnny-cakes round in the bend.

CLICK GO THE SHEARS

Out on the board the old shearer stands,
Grasping his shears in his thin bony hands;
Fixed is his gaze on a bare-bellied yoe
Glory if he gets her, won't he make the ringer go.

Chorus:
Click go the shears boys, click, click, click,
Wide is his blow and his hands move quick,
The ringer looks around and is beaten by a blow,
And curses the old snagger with the bare-bellied yoe.

In the middle of the floor in his cane bottomed chair
Sits the boss of the board with his eyes everywhere,
Notes well each fleece as it comes to the screen,
Paying strict attention that it's taken off clean.

The colonial experience man, he is there of course,
With his shiny leggin's on, just got off his horse
Gazes all around him like a real connoisseur,
Scented soap, and brilliantine and smelling like a whore.

The tar-boy is there waiting in demand
With his blackened tar-pot, in his tarry hand,
Spies one old sheep with a cut upon its back
Hears what he's waiting for it's 'Tar here, Jack!'

Now the shearing is all over, we've all got our cheques
So roll up your swags and it's off down the track,
The first pub we come to it's there we'll have a spree
And everyone that comes along it's 'Have a drink with me.'

There we leave him standing shouting for all hands,
Whilst all around him every 'shouter' stands,
His eye is on the keg which now is lowering fast,
He works hard, he drinks hard, and goes to Hell at last!

With the exception of Waltzing Matilda, this is the best known and most popular of
Australian traditional songs. The word yoe means ewe – was it invented to make the
rhyme in the first verse?

ONE OF THE HAS-BEENS

I'm one of the has-beens, a shearer I mean,
I once was a ringer and used to shear clean;
I could make the wool roll off easy,
Like soil from the plough,
But you may not believe me, because I can't do it now.

Chorus:
I'm as awkward as a new chum,
And used to the frown,
That the boss often shows me,
Saying 'Keep them blades down.'

I've shorn with Pat Hogan, Bill Bright and Jack Gunn,
Charlie Fergus, Tommy Layton and the great roarin' Dunn.
They brought from the Lachlan
The best they could find,
But not one among them could leave me behind.

Still it's no use complaining, I'll never say die,
Though the days of fast shearing for me have gone by.
I'll just take the world nice and easy,
Shear slowly and clean,
And I merely have told you just what I have been.

SHEARING IN A BAR

My shearing days are over, though I never was a gun:
I could always count my twenty at the end of every run.
I used the old Trade Union shears, and the blades were running full
As I shoved them to the knockers and I pushed away the wool.
I shore at Goorianawa and never got the sack;
From Breeza out to Comprador I always could go back;
But though I am a truthful man I find, when in a bar,
That my tally's always doubled but – I never call for tar!

Now shearing on the Western Plains, where the fleece is full of sand
And clover-burr and cork-screw grass, is the place to try your hand;
For the sheep are tough and wiry where they feed on the Mitchell grass,
And every second one of them is close to the 'cobbler' class;
And a pen chocked full of 'cobblers' is a shearer's dream of hell,
And loud and lurid are their words when they catch one on the bell:
But when we're pouring down the grog you'll hear no call for tar,
For the shearer never cuts them – when he's shearing in a bar!

At Louth I got the bell-sheep, a wrinkly tough-woolled brute,
Who never stopped his kicking till I tossed him down the 'chute.
Though my wrist was aching badly, I fought him all the way:
I couldn't afford to miss a blow – I must earn my pound a day;
So when I took a strip of skin, I would hide it with my knee –
Gently turn the sheep around so the right bower couldn't see,
Then try to catch the rousy's eye, and softly whisper, 'Tar';
But it never seems to happen – when I'm shearing in a bar!

I shore away the belly-wool, and trimmed the crutch and hocks,
Then opened up along the neck, while the rousy swept the locks.
Then smartly swung the sheep around, and dumped him on his rear –
Two blows to chip away the wig – (I also took an ear!)
Then down around the shoulder and the blades were opened wide,
As I drove them on the long blow and down the whipping side;
And when I tossed him down the 'chute he was nearly black with tar,
But it never seems to happen – when I'm shearing in a bar!

Now when the season's ended and my grandsons all come back
In their *Vanguards* and their *Holdens* – I was always 'on the track' –
They come and take me into town to fill me up with beer,
And I sit on a corner-stool and listen to them shear:
There's not a bit of difference! It must make the angels weep,
To hear a mob of shearers in a bar-room shearing sheep;
The sheep go rattling down the race and there's never a call for tar,
For they still don't seem to cut them – when they're shearing in the bar!

Then memories come crowding and they roll away the years,
And my hands begin to tighten and they seem to feel the shears:
I want to tell them of the sheds, of sheds where I have shorn,
Full fifty years, or maybe more, before the boys were born.
I want to speak of Yarragreen, Dunlop or Wingadee,
But the beer has started working and I find I cannot see.
So I'd better not start shearing – I'd be bound to call for tar;
Then be treated like a blackleg – when I'm shearing in a bar!

H. P. ('Duke') Tritton

The story goes that this song was written as a co-operative bar-room effort. The 'Duke'
started the ball rolling and the assembled drinkers added the rest, originally to the tune of
'When Irish Eyes are Smiling'.

THE SWAGLESS SWAGGIE

This happened in the years gone by before the bush was cleared,
When every man was six foot high and wore a heavy beard;
One very hot and windy day along the old coach road,
Towards Joe Murphy's wayside pub a bearded stranger strode.

He was a huge and hairy man well over six foot high,
An old slouch hat was on his head and murder in his eye;
No billycan was in his hand, no heavy swag he bore,
But deep and awful were the oaths that swagless swaggie swore.

They were a rough and ready lot, the bushmen gathered there,
But every man was stricken dumb to hear that stranger swear;
He cursed the bush, he cursed mankind and all the universe,
It froze their very blood to hear that swagless swaggie curse.

'I met the Ben Hall gang,' he said, 'the bastards stuck me up,
They pinched me billy, pinched me swag, they pinched me flamin' pup;
They turned me pockets inside out and took me only quid,
I never thought they'd pinch me pipe, but s'elp me God they did.

'I never done the gang no harm, I thought 'em decent chaps;
But now I wouldn't raise a hand to save 'em from the traps;
I'm done forever with the bush, I'm makin' for the town,
Where they won't stick a swaggie up and take a swaggie down.'

The bushmen were a decent lot, as bushmen mostly are,
They filled the stranger up with beer, the hat went round the bar;
The shearers threw some blankets in to make another swag,
The rousers gave a billycan and brand new tucker bag.

Joe Murphy gave a briar pipe he hadn't smoked for years,
The stranger was too full for words, his eyes were dim with tears;
The ringer shouted drinks all round, and then to top it up,
The shearers' cook, the babbling brook, gave him a kelpie pup.

Next day an hour before the dawn, the stranger took the track,
Complete with pup and billycan, his swag upon his back;
Along the most forsaken roads, intent on dodging graft,
He headed for the great north-west, and laughed and laughed and laughed.

Edward Harrington

A THOUSAND MILES AWAY

Hurrah for the old stock saddle,	Knee deep in grass we have to pass,
Hurrah for the stockwhip too,	The truth I'm bound to tell,
Hurrah for the baldy pony	Where in three weeks the cattle get
That will carry me westward ho,	As fat as they can swell,
Carry me westward ho, me boys,	As fat as they can swell me boys
That's where the cattle stray,	A thousand pounds they weigh
On the far Barcoo where they eat nardoo,	On the far Barcoo where they eat nardoo,
A thousand miles away.	A thousand miles away.

Chorus:

So give your horses rein	No Yankee hide ever grew outside
It's across the open plain,	Such beef as we can freeze,
We'll crack our whips like thunderbolts,	Nor Yankee pastures feed such steers
Don't care what some folks say,	As we send overseas.
And running we'll bring home,	As we send overseas me boys,
The cattle that now roam	In shipments every day,
On the far Barcoo and the Flinders too,	From the far Barcoo where they eat nardoo,
A thousand miles away.	A thousand miles away.

So put me up with a snaffle
And a four or five inch spur
And fourteen feet of greenhide whip
To chop the flamin' fur,
I'll yard them snuffy cattle
In a way that's safe to swear –
Will make the overlander
Sit back in his saddle and stare.

This song gives testimony to the immense distances covered by an overlander with a mob of cattle. A thousand miles may not mean much by road train, but a drive from central Queensland to market in Brisbane could mean six months in the saddle. No wonder drovers looked forward to the spree!

CLANCY OF THE OVERFLOW

I had written him a letter which I had, for want of better
Knowledge, sent to where I met him down the Lachlan, years ago;
He was shearing when I knew him, so I sent the letter to him,
Just on spec, addressed as follows, 'Clancy of The Overflow.'

And an answer came directed in a writing unexpected
(And I think the same was written with a thumb-nail dipped in tar):
'Twas his shearing mate who wrote it, and *verbatim* I will quote it:
'Clancy's gone to Queensland droving, and we don't know where he are.'

In my wild erratic fancy visions come to me of Clancy
Gone a-droving 'down the Cooper' where the Western drovers go;
As the stock are slowly stringing, Clancy rides behind them singing,
For the drover's life has pleasures that the townsfolk never know.

And the bush has friends to meet him, and their kindly voices greet him
In the murmur of the breezes and the river on its bars,
And he sees the vision splendid of the sunlit plains extended,
And at night the wondrous glory of the everlasting stars.

I am sitting in my dingy little office, where a stingy
Ray of sunlight struggles feebly down between the houses tall,
And the foetid air and gritty of the dusty, dirty city,
Through the open window floating, spreads its foulness over all.

And in place of lowing cattle, I can hear the fiendish rattle
Of the tramways and the buses making hurry down the street;
And the language uninviting of the gutter children fighting
Comes fitfully and faintly through the ceaseless tramp of feet.

And the hurrying people daunt me, and their pallid faces haunt me
As they shoulder one another in their rush and nervous haste,
With their eager eyes and greedy, and their stunted forms and weedy,
For townsfolk have no time to grow, they have no time to waste.

And I somehow rather fancy that I'd like to change with Clancy,
Like to take a turn at droving where the seasons come and go,
While he faced the round eternal of the cash-book and the journal –
But I doubt he'd suit the office, Clancy of The Overflow.

A. B. ('Banjo') Paterson

And Clancy of The Overflow came down to lend a hand,
No better horseman ever held the reins.
The Man from Snowy River by A. B.('Banjo')Paterson

THE OVERLANDER

There's a trade you all know well,
It's bringing the cattle over.
Now listen, while I tell to you
How I became a drover.
I wanted stock for Queensland –
To Kempsey I did wander
Bought a thousand cattle there,
And then turned overlander.

Chorus:
Pass the bottle round boys,
And don't you leave it stand there,
For tonight we'll drink the health
Of every overlander.

When the cattle were counted
And the outfit ready to start,
I saw the boys all mounted
With their swags thrown in the cart,
All kinds of men I had too
From France and Spain and Flanders –
Lawyers, doctors, good and bad,
In the mob of overlanders.

From the track I then spread out
Where the grass was green and young,
When a squatter with a curse and shout,
Told me to move along.
I said, 'Come draw it mild man,
And don't you raise my dander
For I'm a regular knowin' card,
A Queensland overlander.'

We move the cattle fifty miles
And make camp for the day,
We talk about the rich folk's life
And true loves far away.
Our tucker isn't fancy –
Beef and tea and damper
But wash it down with Queensland rum –
It suits the overlander.

Our clothes are getting dirtier
And throats they choke with dust,
We set our tired horses free
And in the dogs we trust.
We gaze into the shimmering haze,
And dream of places grander,
But, come what may, we know we'll stay –
The Queensland overlander.

I would scorn to prig a shirt,
That all my mates can say
But if we pass a township
Upon a washing day,
The dirty brats of kids would shout,
And quickly raise my dander
Crying, 'Mother dear, take in your clothes,
Here comes the overlander.'

In town we dress ourselves up
And we go and see a play.
We never think of being hard up,
Or how to spend a day,
We steer up to them pretty girls
That dress themselves in grandeur
And while they sweat our cheques, they swear
They love the overlander.

BALLAD OF BEN HALL'S GANG

Come all you wild colonials and listen to my tale;
And a story of bushranging deeds to you I will unveil.
'Tis of those gallant heroes, game fighters one and all –
And we'll sit and sing, God save the King, Dunn, Gilbert and Ben Hall.

Ben Hall he was a squatter and he owned six hundred head;
A peaceful man he was until arrested by Sir Fred.
His home burned down, his wife cleared out, his cattle perished all.
'They'll not take me a second time,' says the valiant Ben Hall.

John Gilbert was a flashy cove, and John O'Meally too;
With Ben and Bourke and Johnny Vane, they were all comrades true.
They rode into Canowindra and gave a public ball –
'Roll up, roll up, and have a spree,' says Gilbert and Ben Hall.

They made a raid on Bathurst, the pace was getting hot;
But Johnny Vane surrendered after Micky Bourke was shot.
O'Meally at Goimbla did like a hero fall,
'The game is getting lively,' says Gilbert and Ben Hall.

'Next week we'll visit Goulburn and clean the banks out there;
So if you see the peelers just tell them to beware;
And one fine day, to Sydney town we mean to pay a call,
'We'll take the whole damn country,' says Dunn, Gilbert and Ben Hall.

In April 1862, Ben Hall, then twenty-five, had a pretty wife, a young son, and a moderately successful cattle property. Arrested as a suspected accomplice of 'Darkie' Gardiner in a hold-up near Forbes, he was held in gaol for a month before the charges against him were dismissed. He returned to find his wife had run off with a former policeman, taking their son. Hall's home had been burned – by police, neighbours said – and his cattle left to starve in the pens. Thus began the career of the most gallant, tragic and romantic of Australian bushrangers. 'Sir Fred' was Sir Frederick Pottinger, an English baronet whose persecution of Hall and inept handling of the hunt for him, made him a public laughing stock, and led to his dishonourable discharge from the force.

THE STREETS OF FORBES

Come all you Lachlan men and a sorrowful tale I'll tell,
The story of a decent man who through misfortune fell,
His name it was Ben Hall, a man of high renown,
Who was hunted from his station, and was like a dog shot down.

For years he roamed the roads, and he showed the traps some fun,
One thousand pounds was on his head, with Gilbert and Jack Dunn.
Ben parted from his comrades, the outlaws did agree,
To give away bushranging and to cross the briny sea.

Ben went to Goobang Creek, and that was his downfall
For riddled like a sieve was the valiant Ben Hall,
'Twas early in the morning upon the fifth of May
That the seven police surrounded him as fast asleep he lay.

Billy Dargin he was chosen to shoot the outlaw dead,
The troopers then fired madly and they filled him full of lead,
They rolled him in his blanket and strapped him to his prad,
And they led him through the streets of Forbes, to show the prize they had.

Billy Dargin was an Aboriginal tracker used by the police to hunt Ben Hall. Such was
public sympathy for Hall that Dargin became a hated man and was poisoned several years
after Hall's capture.

AT DEAD DINGO

It was blazing hot outside and smothering hot inside the weatherboard and iron shanty at Dead Dingo, a place on the 'cleared road', where there was a pub and a police station, and which was sometimes called 'Roasted' and other times 'Potted' Dingo – nicknames suggested by the everlasting drought and the vicinity of the one-pub township of Tinned Dog.

From the front veranda the scene was straight cleared road, running right and left to outback, and to Bourke (and ankle-deep in the red sand dust for perhaps a hundred miles); the rest blue-grey bush, dust, and the heat-wave blazing across every object.

There were only four in the bar-room, though it was New Year's Day. There weren't many more in the county. The girl sat behind the bar – the coolest place in the shanty – reading 'Deadwood Dick'. On a worn and torn and battered horsehair sofa, which had seen cooler places and better days, lay an awful and healthy example, a bearded swagman, with his arms twisted over his head and his face to the wall, sleeping off the death of the dead drunk. Bill and Jim – shearer and rouseabout – sat at a table playing cards. It was about three o'clock in the afternoon, and they had been gambling since nine – and the greater part of the night before – so they were, probably, in a worse condition morally (and perhaps physically) than the drunken swagman on the sofa.

Close under the bar, in a dangerous place for his legs and tail, lay a sheepdog with a chain attached to his collar and wound round his neck.

Presently a thump on the table, and Bill, unlucky gambler, rose with an oath that would have been savage if it hadn't been drawled.

'Stumped?' inquired Jim.

'Not a blanky, lurid deener!' drawled Bill.

Jim drew his reluctant hands from the cards, his eyes went slowly and hopelessly round the room and out the door. There was something in the eyes of both, except when on the card-table, of the look of a man waking in a strange place.

'Got anything?' asked Jim fingering the cards again.

Bill sucked in his cheeks, collected the saliva with difficulty, and spat out on to the veranda floor.

'That's all I got,' he drawled. 'It's gone now.'

Jim leaned back in his chair, twisted, yawned, and caught sight of the dog.

'That there dog yours?' he asked, brightening.

They had evidently been strangers the day before, or as strange to each other as bushmen can be.

Bill scratched behind his ear, and blinked at the dog. The dog woke suddenly to a flea fact.

'Yes,' drawled Bill, 'he's mine.'

'Well, I'm going outback, and I want a dog,' said Jim, gathering the cards briskly. 'Half a quid agin the dog?'

'Half a quid be – !' drawled Bill. 'Call it a quid?'

'Half a blanky quid!'

'A gory, lurid quid!' drawled Bill desperately, and he stooped over his swag.

But Jim's hands were itching in a ghastly way over the cards.

'All right. Call it a – quid.'

The drunkard on the sofa stirred, showed signs of waking, but died again. Remember this, it might come in useful

Bill sat down to the table once more.

Jim rose first, winner of the dog. He stretched, yawned 'Ah, well!' and shouted drinks. Then he shouldered his swag, stirred the dog up with his foot, unwound the chain, said 'Ah, well – so-long!' and drifted out and along the road towards outback, the dog following with head and tail down.

Bill scored another drink on account of girl-pity for bad luck, shouldered his swag, said 'So-long, Mary!' and drifted out and along the road towards Tinned Dog, on the Bourke side. A long, drowsy half-hour passed – the sort of half-hour that is as long as an hour in the places where days are as long as years, and years hold about as much as days do in other places.

The man on the sofa woke with a start, and looked scared and wild for a moment; then he brought his dusty broken boots to the floor, rested his elbows on his knees, took his unfortunate head between his hands, and came back to life gradually.

He lifted his head, looked at the girl across the top of the bar, and formed with his lips, rather than spoke, the words:

'Put up a drink?'

She shook her head tightly and went on reading.

He staggered up, and leaning on the bar, made desperate distress signals with hand, eyes, and mouth.

'No!' she snapped. 'I means no when I says no! You've had too many last drinks already, and the boss says you ain't to have another. If you swear again, or bother me, I'll call him.'

He hung sullenly on the counter for a while, then lurched to his swag, and shouldered it hopelessly and wearily. Then he blinked round, whistled, waited a moment, went on to the front veranda, peered round through the heat and bloodshot eyes and whistled again. He turned and started through to the back door.

'What the devil do you want now?' demanded the girl, interrupted in her reading for the third time by him. 'Stampin' all over the house. You can't go through there! It's privit! I do wish to goodness you'd git!'

'Where the blazes that there dog o' mine got to?' he muttered. 'Did you see a dog?'

'No! What do I want with your dog?'

He whistled out in front again, and round each corner. Then he came back with a decided step and tone.

'Look here! that there dog was lyin' there agin the wall when I went to sleep. He wouldn't stir from me, or my swag, in a year, if he wasn't dragged. He's been blanky well touched, and I wouldn'ter lost him for a fiver. Are you sure you ain't seen a dog?' Then suddenly, as the thought struck him: 'Where's them two chaps that was playin' cards when I wenter sleep?'

'Why!' exclaimed the girl, without thinking, 'there was a dog, now I come to think of it, but I thought it belonged to one of them chaps. Anyway, they played for it, and the other chap won it and took it away.'

He stared at her blankly, with thunder gathering in the blankness.

'What sort of a dog was it?'

Dog described; the chain round the neck settled it.

He scowled at her darkly.

'Now, look here,' he said, 'you've allowed gamblin' in this bar – your boss has. You've got no right to let spielers gamble away a man's dog. Is a customer to lose his dog every time he has a doze to suit your boss? I'll go straight across to the police camp and put you away, and I don't care if you lose your licence. I ain't goin' to lose my dog. I wouldn'ter taken a ten-pound note for that blanky dog! I –'

She was filling a pewter hastily.

'Here! for God's sake have a drink an' stop yer row.'

He drank with satisfaction. Then he hung on the bar with one elbow and scowled out the door.

'Which blanky way did them chaps go?' he growled.

'The one that took the dog went towards Tinned Dog.'

'And I'll haveter go all the blanky way back after him, and most likely lose me shed! Here!' jerking the empty pewter across the bar, 'fill that up again; I'm narked properly, I am, and I'll take twenty-four blanky hours to cool down now. I wouldn'ter lost that dog for twenty quid.'

He drank again with deeper satisfaction, then he shuffled out, muttering, swearing, and threatening louder every step, and took the track to Tinned Dog.

Now the man, girl, or woman, who told me this yarn has never quite settled it in his or her mind as to who really owned the dog. I leave it to you.

Henry Lawson

ALL FOR ME GROG

Well I am a ramblin' lad, and me story it is sad,
If ever I get to Lachlan I should wonder,
For I spent all me brass in the bottom of the glass,
And across the western plains I must wander.

Chorus:
And it's all for me grog, me jolly, jolly grog,
It's all for me beer and tobacco,
For I spent all me tin in a shanty drinking gin,
Now across the western plains I must wander.

Well I'm stiff, stony broke and I've parted from me moke,
And the sky is lookin' black as flamin' thunder;
The shanty boss is blue 'cause I haven't got a sou,
That's the way they treat you when you're down and under.

I'm crook in the head and I haven't been to bed,
Since first I touched this shanty with me plunder.
I see centipedes and snakes, and I'm full of aches and shakes,
And I think it's time to push for way out yonder.

I'll take to the Old Man Plain, and criss-cross him once again,
Until me eyes the track no longer see, boys;
And me beer and whisky brain search for sleep, but all in vain,
And I feel as if I've had the Darling Pea, boys.

So it's hang yer jolly grog, yer hocussed shanty grog,
The beer that is loaded with tobacco;
Graftin' humour I am in, and I'll stick the peg right in
And settle down once more to some hard yakka.

It was common for isolated shanties and pubs to have a back room set aside for the drunk to sleep off the 'horrors', the centipedes and the headaches. The publican also used this frugal and bare abode for the malicious practice of 'lambing down' his clients. A drinker with a healthy roll was given alcohol loaded with substances such as tobacco, which tended to render the tired bushman quickly unconscious. Upon awakening, the poor man, broke again, would be told how he had skulled half a pint of rum, shouted the bar three times, climbed on the bar to sing a song, and had fallen off and knocked himself unconscious. He had no choice but to accept it, scrounge what he could and stagger on his way.

There are many songs inspired by this sort of experience – coming from a world where leisure was truly 'all for me grog'.

LAZY HARRY'S

Well we start - ed out from Ro - to when the sheds had all cut
out, And with whips and whips of rhi - no we meant to push a -
bout, With a three spot cheque be - tween us and Syd - ney in our
eye But we camped at La - zy Har - ry's on the road to Gun - da - gai.
CHORUS
And we camped at La - zy Har - ry's on the road to Gun - da -
gai, The road to Gun - da - gai not five miles from Gun - da - gai,
Yes we camped at La - zy Har - ry's on the road to Gun - da - gai.

We started out from Roto when the sheds had all cut out,
And with whips and whips of rhino that we meant to push about,
With a three spot cheque between us and Sydney in our eye
But we camped at Lazy Harry's on the road to Gundagai.

Chorus:
And we camped at Lazy Harry's on the road to Gundagai,
The road to Gundagai, not five miles from Gundagai,
Yes, we camped at Lazy Harry's on the road to Gundagai.

We crossed the Murrumbidgee near old Yanko in a week
We passed through old Narrandera and crossed the Burnett creek,
And we never stopped at Wagga for we'd Sydney in our eye
And we camped at Lazy Harry's on the road to Gundagai.

We threw our flamin' swags off, and marched into the bar
We ordered rum and raspberry, and a shilling each cigar,
The girl that served the poison, she winked at me so sly
So we camped at Lazy Harry's on the road to Gundagai.

Well I seen lots of girls, me boys, and I've drunk lots of beer
I've met with some of both, me lads, that left me feeling queer,
But for beer to knock you sideways and girls to make you sigh
You should camp at Lazy Harry's on the road to Gundagai.

In a week our spree was over and our cheque was all knocked down
We shouldered our matildas and headed out of town,
The girls stood us a nobbler, as we sadly waved goodbye
And we tramped from Lazy Harry's on the road to Gundagai.

Last chorus:
And we tramped from Lazy Harry's on the road to Gundagai,
The road to Gundagai, not five miles from Gundagai,
Yes, we tramped from Lazy Harry's on the road to Gundagai.

The original site of the pub was flooded by the Snowy Mountains Scheme (probably a good thing too!). We were told that Harry was too fat and lazy to tie his shoelaces and had to kick his shoes out in front of him one at a time, and catch up with them.

THE SHEARER'S DREAM

I dreamt I shore in a shearin' shed,
And it was a dream of joy,
For every one of the rouseabouts
Was a girl dressed up as a boy –
Dressed up like a page in a pantomime,
The prettiest ever seen –
They had flaxen hair, they had coal-black hair,
And every shade between.

The shed was cooled by electric fans
That was one over every shoot;
The pens was of polished ma-ho-gany,
And everything else to suit;
The huts had springs to the mattresses,
And the tucker was simply grand,
And every night by the billabong
We danced to a German band.

Our pay was the wool off the jumbuck's back,
So we shore till all was blue –
The sheep was washed afore they were shore
(And the rams was scented too);
And we all of us wept when the shed cut out,
In spite of the long, hot days,
For every hour them girls waltzed in
With whisky and beer on trays!

There was three of them girls to every chap,
And as jealous as they could be –
There was three of them girls to every chap,
And six of 'em picked on me;
We was draftin' 'em out for the homeward track
And sharin' 'em round like steam,
When I awoke with my head in the blazin' sun
To find 'twas a shearer's dream.

Henry Lawson

FLASH JACK FROM GUNDAGAI

I've shore at Burrabogie, and I've shore at Toganmain,
I've shore at big Willandra and out on the Coleraine,
But before the shearing was over, I wished myself back again
A-shearing for old Tom Patterson on the One Tree Plain.

Chorus:
All among the wool boys, all among the wool,
Keep your wide blades full boys, keep your wide blades full,
I can do a respectable tally myself, whenever I likes to try,
They know me round the country as Flash Jack from Gundagai.

I've shore at big Willandra and I've shore at Tilberoo,
And once I drew my blades boys upon the famed Barcoo,
At Cowan Downs and Trida, as far as Moulamein,
But I was always glad to get back again to the One Tree Plain.

I've pinked 'em with the Wolseleys and rushed with B-bows too
And shaved 'em in the grease my lads, with the grass seeds showing through,
But I never slummed my pen, my lads, whatever it might contain,
While shearing for old Tom Patterson on the One Tree Plain.

I've been whalin' up the Lachlan, and I've dossed on Cooper's Creek,
And once I rung Cudjingie shed, and I blued it in a week.
But when Gabriel blows his trumpet, I'll catch the morning train,
And push for old Tom Patterson's on the One Tree Plain.

ANDY'S GONE WITH CATTLE

Our Andy's gone with cattle now –
Our hearts are out of order –
With drought he's gone to battle now
Across the Queensland border.

He's left us in dejection now,
Our thoughts with him are roving;
It's dull on this selection now,
Since Andy went a-droving.

Who now shall wear the cheerful face
In times when things are slackest?
And who shall whistle round the place
When Fortune frowns her blackest?

Oh, who shall cheek the squatter now
When he comes round us snarling?
His tongue is growing hotter now
Since Andy crossed the Darling.

Oh, may the showers in torrents fall,
And all the tanks run over;
And may the grass grow green and tall
In pathways of the drover;

And may good angels send the rain
On desert stretches sandy;
And when the summer comes again
God grant 'twill bring us Andy.

Henry Lawson

BILLY OF TEA

D   G   D
You can talk of your whis-ky, talk of your beer, There's some-thing much
E 7   A 7   D
ni - cer that's wait - ing us here, It sits on the fire be -
G   D   G   CHORUS same tune as Verse   A 7   D
neath the gum tree, There's no-thing much ni - cer than a bil -ly of tea.

Tom Blackman's Waltz
D   A 7   Em   A 7   D
A 7   D   G   Em   A 7
D
G   E 7   A 7   D   A   D
G   E 7   A 7   D

You can talk of your whisky, talk of your beer,
There's something much nicer that's waiting us here,
It sits on the fire beneath the gum tree,
There's nothing much nicer than a billy of tea.

So fill up your tumbler as high as you can
And don't you dare tell me it's not the best plan,
You can let all your beer and your spirits go free –
I'll stick to my darling old billy of tea.

I rise in the morning as soon as it's light
And go to the nose bag to see it's alright,
That the ants on the sugar no mortgage have got
And straight away sling my old black billy-pot.

And while it is boiling the horses I seek
And follow them down, as far as the creek,
I take off their hobbles and let them run free
Then haste to tuck into my billy of tea.

And at night when I camp if the day has been warm
I give to my horses their tucker of corn,
From the two in the pole to the one in the lead
A billy for each holds a comfortable feed.

Then the fire I make and the water I get
And corned beef and damper, in order, I set,
But I don't touch the grub though so hungry I be –
I wait till it's ready – the billy of tea.

BOILING THE BILLY

The 'billy' is a tin can, to which a wire handle is attached. Born in Australia, and unique in its simplicity, it is a comfort to a traveller, and is a burden to no man or woman.

The term may come from the Aboriginal 'billa', meaning water, or creek – hence billabong, but maybe relates to the 'chapman's billy' immortalised in the poem 'Tam O'Shanter' by Robert Burns. In Scotland, the chapman is a peddler, and the billy is his comrade, or mate. And to many a lonely traveller the billy proved to be his most constant mate, and bearer of his chief delight – a cup of billy tea.

> 'I turn the slip jack, make the tea,
> All's as still, as still can be –
> And the old black billy winks at me.'

After a solid morning's work, or a long day's hike, when the meal is over, boil the billy and experience tea, which at its worst, will be good. Billy is famous, and those who have slept out in the bush, and boiled brew after brew to complete the breakfast, will know what is meant when we say that billy tea is full of flavour, and one of the last true luxuries left in this world.

Cheap, light and useful, the billy is a fine testament to home-grown ingenuity, a gift from a world where people were isolated by distance, and equipment was scarce. In the past 'she' has figured in many a comedy and tragedy and has been the repository of the last words of many a perished swagman.

Individuals take pride in their cup of tea, and there are various ways of boiling the billy. You can erect a pair of forked sticks and sling the billy over the fire on a crosspiece; this is a good plan for a permanent fireplace. Or simply sit the billy into the side of a hot fire, resting it in the coals. Always fill the billy to the brim, or over the years the rim will burn away. Leave the lid off so that the water can take on a smokey flavour. At this point the water is worth considering: river water boils faster than rain water, still water quicker than running water, and city tap water is definitely to be avoided. It has a bad taste.

When the water is boiling vigorously throw in the tea and remove the billy from the fire. A comfortable palm-full of ordinary everyday tea will suffice in a four-pint billy, but you should vary the amount for personal taste. Allow to stand for a few minutes, tap the side with a stick – watch the leaves sink to the bottom. Pour directly from the billy into the tin mug, and drink it black.

For an extra treat, take a small bunch of young gum leaves, and immerse for several seconds. Tap, and pour. The tea will have just that hint of eucalyptus in the after-taste, and is a fine drop.

Billy tea is better than pot-made tea because the leaves infuse in water that is actually boiling, because the quality of heat produced by wood is superior to that produced by either gas or electricity, and this quality is transferred to the drink, and because . . . well, it just is!

MICKETY MULGA

He worked wid us at Wantigong –
Old Mickety Mulga Jim.
We'd all a-gone blue mouldy if
It 'adn't bin for him.
He'd keep us yarnin' at the fire,
An' larfin' be the hour
At 'is emusin' annikdotes,
Be George, he 'ad a power.
'E told us up in Queensland, where
'E'd never go again,
He come to some dry water-'ole
Upon a ten mile plain.
The tank was dry, and Jim was dry,
But be a 'appy thought,
He wrung 'e's empty water-bag
An' got about a quart;
But couldn't find a stick o' wood
To bile his billy by,
So stuck a match into the grass,
Which then was pretty dry.
He 'eld the billy to the flame
Wid a bit of fencing wire,
But 'ad to go to foller it,
So rapid run the fire.
Five miles acrost that flamin' plain
He raced that fire, did he,
But when at last the billy biled,
He 'ad forgot the tea!

T. Ranken

FOUR LITTLE JOHNNY-CAKES

Hurrah for the Lachlan boys, and join me in a cheer,
For that's the place to go and make a good cheque every year.
With a toadskin in me pocket, that I borrowed off a friend,
And isn't it nice and cosy to be campin' in the bend.

Chorus:
With me little brown flour bag a-sittin' on the stump,
Me little tea and sugar bag a-lookin' nice and plump,
I've a nice fat codfish, just off the hook,
And four little Johnny-cakes –
A credit to the cook.

I've got half a loaf of bread, and some praties that I shook,
And perhaps a bit of brownie that I snaffled off the cook.
I've a nice leg of mutton with a bit cut off the end,
Ah, isn't it nice and cosy, to be camping in the bend?

I've a good supply of books, and some papers to read,
Got plenty of matches and a good supply of weed.
I wouldn't be a squatter as beside me fire I sit,
With me paper in me hands and me old pipe lit.

And when the shearin' time comes, I'll be in me glory then,
I'll saddle up a moke and soon scrounge up a pen.
I'll ride over valleys, gallop o'er the plain,
Shoot a turkey, stick a pig, then I'll be in the bend again.

Last chorus:
With me little brown flour bag a-sittin' on the stump.
Me little tea and sugar bag a-lookin' nice and plump.
I've a nice fat codfish, just off the hook,
And four little Johnny-cakes –
I'm proud to be the cook.

The swaggie's life was one full of simple joys. 'Johnny-cakes' are a crude form of bread, consisting of flour, water and salt, which is baked in the ashes of the fire. The skill required to produce light, edible cakes by this method is rare today; though on occasion we have experienced this damper (as it is more commonly known) to be a real bush treat.

THE LACHLAN TIGERS

At his gate each shearer stood as the whistle loudly blew,
With eyebrows fixed and lips compressed the tigers all bent too;
You could hear the clicking of the shears as through the wool they glide,
You see a gun already turned, he's on the whipping side.

Chorus:
A lot of Lachlan tigers it's plain to see we are,
Hark to our burly ringer as he loudly calls for tar;
'Tar here,' calls one and quick the tar boy flies
'Sweep those locks away,' another loudly cries.

The scene it is a lively one and ought to be admired,
There hasn't been a better board since Jacky Howe expired;
Along the board our gaffer walks his face all in a frown,
And passing by the ringer says, 'You watch my lad, keep down.'

For I must have their bellies off, and topknots too likewise,
My eye is quick so none of your tricks or from me you will fly,
Oh, curses on our gaffer, he's never on our side,
To shear a decent tally boys, in vain I've often tried.

I have a pair of Ward and Paine's that are both bright and new,
I'll rig them up and I'll let you see what I can really do!
For I've shorn on the Riverine where they shear 'em by the score
But such a terror as this to clip I never shore before.

If any shearer wished to confirm his prowess he would boast that he had worked on the Lachlan. His listeners would be well aware that only the best could get a job there. They were, of course, all 'ryebuck' shearers, and could out-shear, out-drink, out-fight and out-love any other two men put together. The most famous 'tiger' was Jacky Howe who set a world record in 1892, when he shore 327 ewes in 7 hours and 20 minutes, with hand shears!

UGLY DAVE

I'm a stock-man by me trade And me name is Ug-ly
Dave, I'm old and grey and I've only got one eye, In the
yard I'm good, of course, But just put me on a horse And I'll
go where lots of oth-ers dare-n't try. I can
lead 'em through the gid-gee, O-ver coun-try rough and rid-gy, I'll
lose 'em in the ve-ry worst of scrub I can
ride both rough and ea-sy, With a dew-drop, I'm a dai-sy; And a
right down bob-by-daz-zler in the pub. 2. You should

I'm a stockman by me trade
And me name is Ugly Dave,
I'm old and grey and I've only got one eye,
In the yard I'm good, of course,
But just put me on a horse
And I'll go where lots of others daren't try.

I can lead 'em through the gidgee,
Over country rough and ridgy,
I'll lose 'em in the very worst of scrub.
I can ride both rough and easy,
With a dewdrop, I'm a daisy;
And a right down bobby-dazzler in the pub.

You should see me with a whip,
I can give the dawdlers gyp,
I can make the flamin' echoes roar and ring,
With a branding iron well,
I'm a perfect flaming swell;
In fact, I'm duke of every bloody thing.

If it's fencing that you're after,
I'm a mighty flamin' grafter
I bar 'em from the bottom of the hole,
Clean-skin fleece they are a treat,
I can chuck 'em fifty feet;
But I wouldn't be a scab to save me soul.

Now see me skin a sheep,
It's so lovely you could weep,
I can act the silvertail as if me blood were blue.
Now strike me pink or dead!
If I stood upon me head,
I'd be just as good as any other two!

I've a notion in me pate,
That it's luck – it isn't fate,
That I'm so far above the common rung
For in anything I do,
You can cut me fair in two,
For I'm much too bloody good to be in one!

THE DROVER'S DREAM

One night while droving sheep, my companions lay asleep,
There was not a star to 'luminate the sky,
I was dreaming I suppose, for my eyes were partly closed,
When a very strange procession passed me by.
First there came a kangaroo, with his swag of blankets blue,
A dingo ran beside him as a mate;
They were travelling mighty fast,
But they shouted as they passed:
'We'll have to jog along, it's getting late.'

The pelican and the crane they came in from off the plain
To amuse the company with a Highland fling;
The dear old bandicoot played the tune upon his flute,
And the native bears sat round them in a ring.
The brolga and the crow sang us songs of long ago,
The frill-necked lizard listened with a smile,
And the emu standing near
With his claw up to his ear
Said, 'That's the funniest thing I've heard for quite a while.'

The frogs from out the swamp where the atmosphere is damp
Came bounding in and sat upon some stones;
They all unrolled their swags and produced from little bags
The violin, the banjo and the bones.
The goanna and the snake and the adder, wide awake
With an alligator danced the Soldier's Joy;
In the spreading silky oak
The jackass cracked a joke,
And the magpie sang The Wild Colonial Boy.

Some wombats darted out from the ti-tree all about,
And performed a set of Lancers very well;
The parrot green and blue gave the orchestra its cue
To strike up the Old Log Cabin in the Dell.
I was dreaming I suppose of these entertaining shows,
But it never crossed my mind I was asleep,
Till the boss beneath the cart
Woke me up with such a start
Yellin' 'Dreamy, where the hell are all the sheep?'

LIONEL LINDSAY

HOW M^cDOUGAL TOPPED THE SCORE

A peaceful spot is Piper's Flat. The folk that live around –
They keep themselves by keeping sheep and turning up the ground;
But the climate is erratic, and the consequences are
The struggle with the elements is everlasting war.
We plough, and sow, and harrow – then sit down and pray for rain;
And then we all get flooded out and have to start again.
But the folk are now rejoicing as they ne'er rejoiced before,
For we've played Molongo cricket, and McDougal topped the score!

Molongo had a head on it, and challenged us to play
A single-innings match for lunch – the losing team to pay;
We were not great guns at cricket, but we couldn't well say no,
So we all began to practise, and we let the reaping go.
We scoured the Flat for ten miles round to muster up our men,
But when the list was totalled we could only number ten.
Then up spoke big Tim Brady: he was always slow to speak,
And he said – 'What price McDougal, who lives down at Cooper's Creek?'

So we sent for old McDougal, and he stated in reply
That he'd never played at cricket, but he'd half a mind to try.
He couldn't come to practise – he was getting in his hay,
But he guessed he'd show the beggars from Molongo how to play.
Now, McDougal was a Scotchman, and a canny one at that,
So he started in to practise with a paling for a bat.
He got Mrs Mac to bowl to him, but she couldn't run at all,
So he trained his sheep-dog, Pincher, how to scout and fetch the ball.

Now, Pincher was no puppy; he was old, and worn, and grey;
But he understood McDougal, and – accustomed to obey –
When McDougal cried out 'Fetch it!' he would fetch it in a trice,
But, until the word was 'Drop it!' he would grip it like a vice.
And each succeeding night they played until the light grew dim:
Sometimes McDougal struck the ball – sometimes the ball struck him.
Each time he struck, the ball would plough a furrow in the ground;
And when he missed, the impetus would turn him three times round.

The fatal day at last arrived – the day that was to see
Molongo bite the dust, or Piper's Flat knocked up a tree!
Molongo's captain won the toss, and sent his men to bat,
And they gave some leather-hunting to the men of Piper's Flat.
When the ball sped where McDougal stood, firm planted in his track,
He shut his eyes, and turned him round, and stopped it with his back!
The highest score was twenty-two, the total sixty-six,
When Brady sent a yorker down that scattered Johnson's sticks.

Then Piper's Flat went in to bat, for glory and renown,
But, like the grass before the scythe, our wickets tumbled down.
'Nine wickets down, for seventeen, with fifty more to win!'
Our captain heaved a sigh, and sent McDougal in.
'Ten pounds to one you'll lose it!' cried a barracker from town;
But McDougal said, 'I'll tak' it, mon!' and planted the money down.
Then he girded up his moleskins in a self-reliant style,
Threw off his hat and boots and faced the bowler with a smile.

He held the bat the wrong side out, and Johnson with a grin
Stepped lightly to the bowling crease, and sent a 'wobbler' in;
McDougal spooned it softly back, and Johnson waited there,
But McDougal, crying *Fetch it!* started running like a hare.
Molongo shouted 'Victory! He's out as sure as eggs,'
When Pincher started through the crowd, and ran through Johnson's legs.
He seized the ball like lightning; then he ran behind a log.
And McDougal kept on running, while Molongo chased the dog!

They chased him up, they chased him down, they chased him round, and then
He darted through the slip-rail as the scorer shouted 'Ten!'
McDougal puffed; Molongo swore; excitement was intense;
As the scorer marked down twenty, Pincher cleared a barbed-wire fence.
'Let us head him!' shrieked Molongo. 'Brain the mongrel with a bat!'
'Run it out! Good old McDougal!' yelled the men of Piper's Flat.
And McDougal kept on jogging, and then Pincher doubled back,
And the scorer counted *Forty* as they raced across the track.

McDougal's legs were going fast, Molongo's breath was gone –
But still Molongo chased the dog – McDougal struggled on.
When the scorer shouted *'Fifty',* then they knew the chase could cease;
And McDougal gasped out 'Drop it!' as he dropped within his crease.
Then Pincher dropped the ball, and as instinctively he knew
Discretion was the wiser plan, he disappeared from view;
And as Molongo's beaten men exhausted lay around
We raised McDougal shoulder-high, and bore him from the ground.

We bore him to McGinniss's where lunch was ready laid,
And filled him up with whisky-punch, for which Molongo paid.
We drank his health in bumpers and we cheered him three times three,
And when Molongo got its breath Molongo joined the spree.
And the critics say they never saw a cricket match like that,
When McDougal broke the record in the game at Piper's Flat;
And the folk are jubilating as they never did before;
For we played Molongo cricket – and McDougal topped the score!

Thomas E. Spencer

BLUEY BRINK

There once was a shearer, by name Bluey Brink
A devil for work and a devil for drink;
He could shear his two hundred a day without fear,
And drink without winking, four gallons of beer.

Now Jimmy the barman who served out the drink,
He hated the sight of this 'ere Bluey Brink,
For he stayed much too late, and he came much too soon;
At evening, at morning, at night and at noon.

One morning as Jimmy was cleaning the bar,
With sulphuric acid he kept in a jar,
In comes the shearer a-howlin' with thirst,
'Whatever you got Jim, just give me that first.'

Now it ain't in the histories, it ain't in the print,
But Bluey drank acid with never a wink
Saying, 'That's the stuff Jimmy! Why strike me stone dead,
This'll make me the ringer of Stephenson's shed!'

All that long day as he served out the beer,
Jim's legs were a-tremblin' and he shook with the fear;
Too worried to argue, too anxious to fight,
Seeing the shearer a corpse by the night.

Early next morning as he opened the bar,
In came old Bluey a-howlin' for more
With his eyebrows all singed and his whiskers deranged,
And holes in his hide like a dog with the mange.

Says Jimmy to Bluey, 'How'd you like me new stuff?'
Says Bluey, 'It's fine, but I ain't had enough,
It gives me great courage to shear and to fight,
But why does the stuff set me whiskers alight?

'I thought I knew drink, but I must have been wrong,
That stuff wot you gave me was proper and strong;
It set me to coughin', and you know I'm no liar –
Each bloody cough set me whiskers on fire!'

Anon.

AUGATHELLA STATION

Farewell and adieu to you Brisbane ladies,
Farewell and adieu to you girls of Toowong.
We've sold all our cattle and it's northwards we'll travel
But we hope we will see you again before long.

Chorus:
We'll rant and we'll roar like true Queensland drovers,
Rant and we'll roar as onwards we push,
Until we return to the Augathella Station
It's flamin' dry goin' through the old Queensland bush.

The first camp we make will be down by the river,
We'll off with our swags, and lay the place flat.
We'll bed down the herd and before the sun rises,
We'll move 'em again and we'll cross the black butt.

Mount your horses, we'll ride into town boys,
We'll stop at the pub, and drink the place dry.
We'll spend all our money on the shanty town women
And as dawn is a-breaking, away we will ride.

The girls are so pretty, they look so enchanting,
Bewitching, graceful, they join in the fun,
With the waltz and the polka and all types of dancing,
To the old concertina of Jack Smith the Don.

So fill up your glasses let's drink to our lasses,
Let's sing the last chorus, sing farewell to all
And if you return to the Augathella Station
Why don't you come by there, and pay us a call?

WHEN THE RAIN TUMBLES DOWN IN JULY

Let me wander north to the homestead,
Way out, further on there to roam,
By a gully in flood let me linger
When the summery sunshine has flown,
Where the logs tangle up on the creek-bed,
And the clouds veil the old northern sky,
And the cattle move back from the lowlands,
When the rain tumbles down in July.

The settlers with sad hearts are watching
The rise of the stream from the dawn.
Their best crops are always in floodreach
If it rises much more they'll be gone.
The cattle string out along the fences
As the breeze from the south races by,
And the limbs from the old gums are falling,
When the rain tumbles down in July.

The old sleeping gums by the river
Awaken to herds straying by
From the flats where the fences have vanished
As the storm clouds gather on high.
The wheels of the wagon stop turning
And the stock horse is turned out to stray,
And the old station dogs are a-dozing
On the husks in the barn through the day.

And the drover draws rein by the river
It's been years since he's seen it so high,
And that's just a story of homewards
When the rain tumbles down in July.

Slim Dusty

The experiences of his family and neighbours during the devastating floods of 1946 in
NSW inspired Slim Dusty to write this song. It was his first hit and became his signature
tune for many years. It has become one of our favourites and, to us, evokes the spirit of
Lawson and Paterson in its observation and understanding – there can be no greater
tribute.

ANOTHER FALL OF RAIN

A7   D
Now the weath-er had been sul-try for a
G   D   Bm
fort-night's time or more, The shear-ers had been battl-ing might and
A7   D
main   And some had got the cen-tur-y as
G   D   A7
nev-er had be-fore But now all hands are wait-ing for the
D   CHORUS   G
rain. For the boss is get-ting rust-y, and the
D
ring-er's cav-ing in His band-aged wrist is ach-ing with the
A   D
pain And the se-cond man I swear, will
G   D   A   D
make it hot for him, Un-less we have an-o-ther fall of rain.

Now the weather had been sultry for a fortnight's time or more,
The shearers had been battling might and main,
And some had got the century as never had before
But now all hands are waiting for the rain.

Chorus:
For the boss is getting rusty, and the ringer's caving in
His bandaged wrist is aching with the pain
And the second man I swear, will make it hot for him,
Unless we have another fall of rain.

A few had taken quarters and were coiling in their bunks
When we shore the six-tooth wethers from the plain.
And if the sheep get harder, then a few more men will funk,
Unless we get another fall of rain.

But the sky is clouding over and the thunder's muttering loud,
And the clouds are driving eastwards o'er the plain,
And I see the lightning flashing from the edge of yon black cloud,
And I hear the gentle patter of the rain.

So, lads, put on your stoppers, and let us to the huts
Where we'll gather round and have a friendly game,
While some are playing music and some play ante-up
And some are gazing outwards at the rain.

But now the rain is over, let the pressers spin the screws,
Let the teamsters back the waggons in again,
And we'll block the classer's table by the way we push them through,
For everything is merry since the rain.

And the boss he won't be rusty when his sheep they are all shorn,
And the ringer's wrist won't ache much with the pain
Of pocketing his season's cheque for fifty pounds or more,
And the second man will ride him hard again.

Words based on a poem by John Neilson

There were numerous superstitions developed about the various diseases and complaints (notably rheumatism) that shearers incurred from shearing wet sheep. After a long dry spell with hard wool, the prospect of rain and a 'holiday' in the huts was something to be prayed for.

THE COCKIES OF BUNGAREE

Come all you weary travellers that's out of work, just mind,
Come take a trip to Bungaree, and plenty there you'll find.
Have a trial with the cocky, you can take it straight from me,
You'll very likely rue the day that you first saw Bungaree.

And how I came this weary way, I mean to let you know,
Being out of employment, I didn't know where to go.
I called at the registry office and there I did agree,
To take a job of clearing for the cocky at Bungaree.

Well the first thing Monday morning, mate, it was the usual go,
He called me to my breakfast before the cocks did crow.
The stars were shining gloriously, and the moon was high, you see,
I thought before the sun would rise, I'd die in Bungaree.

And when I went in to supper, 'twas after half-past nine,
And when I had ate it, sure I thought, it was just about bedtime.
But the cocky he came up to me sayin' with a merry laugh:
'I want you for an hour or two, to cut a bit of chaff.'

And after about a week, or more, I reckoned I'd had enough,
So I went straight up to that cocky berk, and asked him for my stuff.
I went straight into Ballaarat, but it didn't last me long,
I marched right into the Railway Hotel, and blew me one pound one.

So come all you weary travellers, that's out of work, just mind,
Come take a trip to Bungaree and plenty there you'll find.
Take a trial with the cocky, and I'm sure you will agree,
You'll very likely rue the day you first saw Bungaree!

A BUSHMAN'S SONG

I'm travellin' down the Castlereagh, and I'm a station-hand,
I'm handy with the ropin' pole, I'm handy with the brand,
And I can ride a rowdy colt, or swing the axe all day,
But there's no demand for a station-hand along the Castlereagh.

Chorus:
It was shift, boys, shift for there wasn't the slightest doubt
We had to make a shift to the stations further out,
With the pack-horse runnin' after, for he follows like a dog,
We must strike across the country at the old jig-jog.

This old black horse I'm riding – if you notice what's his brand,
He wears the crooked R, you see – none better in the land.
He takes a lot of beatin', and the other day we tried,
For a bit of a joke, with a racing bloke, for twenty pounds a side.

Chorus:
It was shift, boys, shift, for there wasn't the slightest doubt
That I had to make him shift, for the money was nearly out;
But he cantered home a winner, with the other one at the flog –
He's a red-hot sort to pick up with his old jig-jog.

I asked a cove for shearin' once along the Marthaguy:
'We shear non-union here,' says he. 'I call it scab,' says I.
I looked along the shearin' floor before I turned to go –
There were eight or ten non-union men a-shearin' in a row.

Chorus:
It was shift, boys, shift, for there wasn't the slightest doubt
It was time to make a shift with the leprosy about,
So I saddled up my horses, and I whistled to my dog,
And I left his scabby station at the old jig-jog.

I went to Illawarra, where my brother's got a farm;
He has to ask his landlord's leave before he lifts his arm,
The landlord owns the countryside – man, woman, dog and cat,
They haven't the cheek to dare to speak without they touch their hat.

Chorus:
It was shift, boys, shift, for there wasn't the slightest doubt
Their little landlord god and I would soon have fallen out;
Was I to touch my hat to him? – was I his bloomin' dog?
So I makes for up the country at the old jig-jog.

But it's time that I was movin', I've a mighty way to go
Till I drink artesian water from a thousand feet below;
Till I meet the overlanders with the cattle comin' down –
And I'll work a while till I makes a pile, then have a spree in town.

Chorus:
So it's shift, boys, shift, for there isn't the slightest doubt
We've got to make a shift to the stations further out;
The pack-horse runs behind us, for he follows like a dog,
And we cross a lot of country at the old jig-jog.

Words by A. B. ('Banjo') Paterson

TOMAHAWKIN' FRED (THE LADIES' MAN)

Some shearing I have done and some prizes I have won
Through my knuckling down so close unto the skin,
But I'd rather tomahawk any day than shear a flock
For that's the only way I'll make some tin.

Chorus:
And I am just about to cut for the Darling,
To turn a hundred out, I know the plan,
Give me sufficient cash, and you'll see me make a splash,
For I'm Tomahawkin' Fred, the ladies' man.

Put me on the shearing floor and it's there I'll bet for sure
That I'll give to any ringer ten sheep start,
For it's on the whipping side it's away from them I glide
Just like a bullet or a dart.

Of me you may have read for I'm Tomahawkin' Fred,
My shearing laurels are known both near and far,
I'm the don of the Riverine, 'midst the shearers cut a shine,
And the tar boys say I never call for tar.

Hove in and go ahead for I'm Tomahawkin' Fred,
On the shearing floor, my boys, I cut a shine;
There is Roberts, and Jack Gunn shearing prizes they have won,
But my tally's never under ninety-nine.

EUABALONG BALL

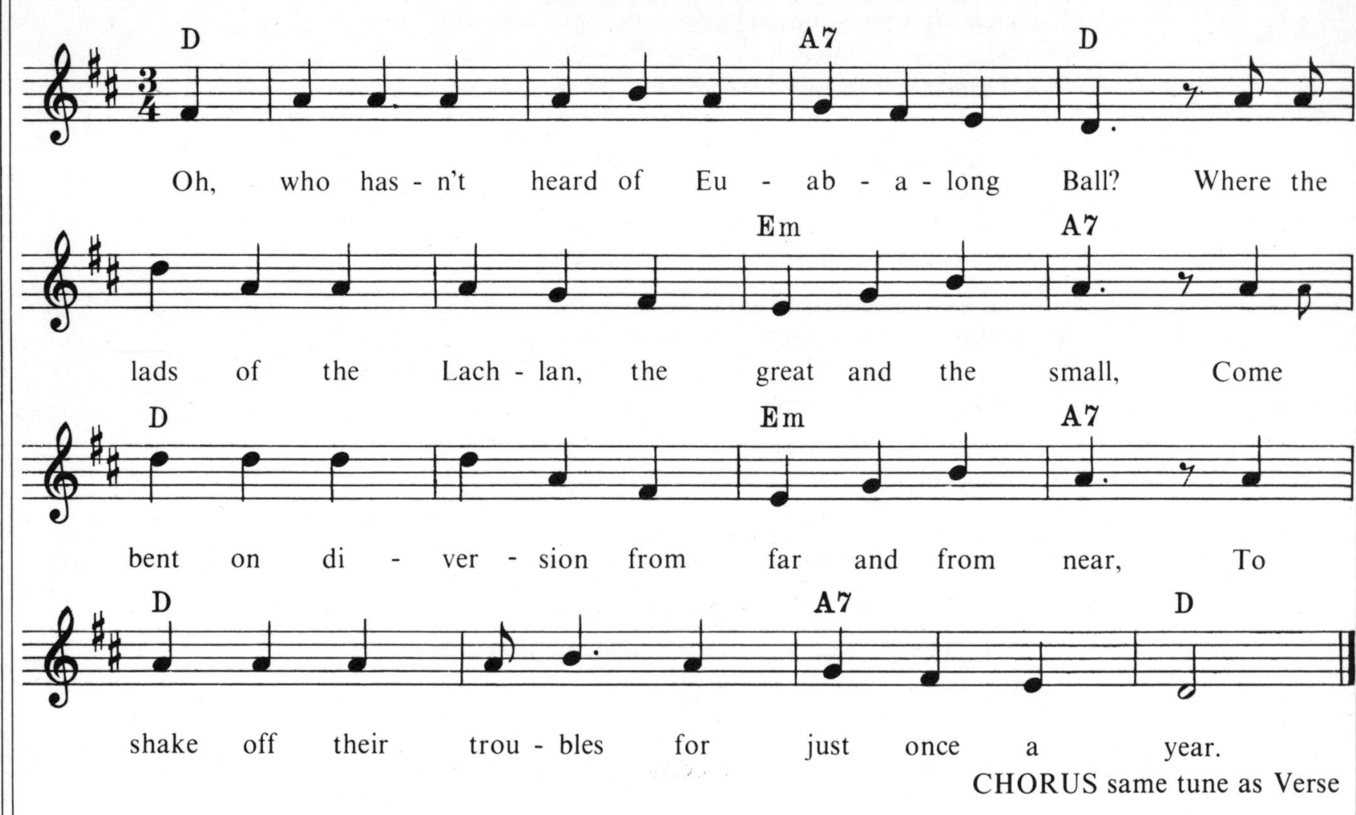

Oh, who hasn't heard of Euabalong Ball?
Where the lads of the Lachlan, the great and the small,
Come bent on diversion, from far and from near,
To shake off their troubles for just once a year.

Chorus:
Euabalong Ball was a wonderful sight,
Where the lads and the lasses were dancing all night,
And it's many a lad who will blush to recall,
The polkas he danced at Euabalong Ball.

The boundary riders were friskin' about,
And the well-sinkers seemed to be feeling the drought.
If the water was scarce, there was whisky to spare,
What they never swallowed, they rubbed in their hair.

There were sheilas in plenty, some two or three score,
Some two-tooths, some weaners and some maybe more.
With their fleeces all scented and fluffy and clean,
Such fine looking shearlings you never have seen.

The music set up and was going a-pace,
Some went at a canter, and some at a race.
There was slippin' and slidin', staggerin' and glidin',
And to vary the pace, there were couples collidin'.

Much hugging and squeezing – of course on the sly –
And tender emotions when bidding goodbye.
And many who shouldn't, but got drunk and stayed,
Woke with a blush of regret, the next day.

THE HEEL AND TOE POLKA

*Repeat Parts 1 and 2 as before, i.e. each twice again.

Embrace in the waltz hold. Form a line around the floor to make a circle, the girls on the outside.

Facing anti-clockwise, hop on your inside leg. Simultaneously, the outside leg is shot forward and, outstretched, lands on the heel. Hop again, the extended leg springs back to rest on the toe – both feet are now together again. This entire movement is repeated, and if you sing 'heel and toe, heel and toe', you'll fall into the rhythm.

Skip forward with four sideways steps.

Now, about face and with the same hold it's – heel and toe, heel and toe (on a new inside leg), skip, two, three, four, back around the circle. Release your partner and each couple clap right hands three times, followed by the left, then both hands and slap your knees (all three times). Swing your partner linking right arms. Half way round you catch the left arm of the new partner until you return to the starting position.

The dance finishes when you have danced with everyone in the circle. The ideal size for this dance is a circle of fifteen couples.
Here's a simple call:

> Heel and toe, heel and toe, skip, two, three, four
> Heel and toe, heel and toe, skip, two, three, four
> Right hand clap,
> Left hand clap,
> Both hands clap,
> Slap your knees,
> Swing on the right, three, four
> Change by the left, three, four

The tune 'Little Brown Jug' is ideal for learning this dance, which is often called the Brown Jug Polka.

THE RYEBUCK SHEARER

Well I come from the south and my name is Field
And when my shears are properly steeled,
It's a hundred or more I have very often peeled,
And of course I'm a ryebuck shearer.

Chorus:
If I don't shear a tally before I go
My shears and stones in the river I'll throw,
And I'll never open Sawbees or take another blow,
Till I prove I'm a ryebuck shearer.

There's a bloke on the board and I heard him say
That I couldn't shear a hundred sheep a day,
But one fine day mate, I'll show him the way
I'll prove I'm a ryebuck shearer.

You ought to see our ringer, he's nothing but a farce
When the cobbler's coming up, he's always first to pass,
As for the shearing, he's more arse than class
And he'll never be a ryebuck shearer.

There's a swaggie down the creek his name is Jack,
He rolled into town with a swag on his back;
He asked us for a job, said he needed a few bob
And he swears he's a ryebuck shearer.

Yes, I'll make a splash, and I won't say when,
I'll up off me arse and I'll into the pen
While the ringer's shearing eight, mate, I'll be shearing ten
And I'll prove I'm a ryebuck shearer.

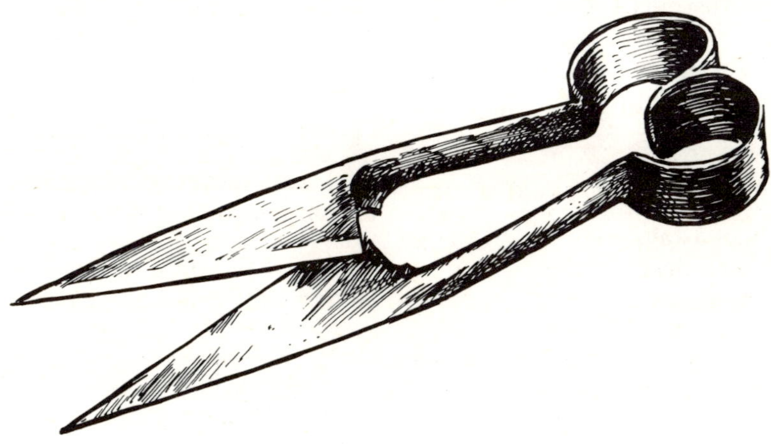

Of all the songs we sing, this is the most popular. Why? It's got an inherent power which
manages to communicate itself to all who hear or sing this shearing classic. To be a
ryebuck shearer you had to be good – if you didn't rate on the shearing floor, you didn't
rate at all. The term specifies a minimum standard in a particular skill, by which the whole
of a man was judged. In our song, of course, we are all ryebuck shearers, and we have
added a couple of verses of our own.

SOUTH AUSTRALIA

Solo: In South Australia I was born –
Chorus: Heave away! haul away!
Solo: South Australia round Cape Horn,
Chorus: Bound for South Australia.

Chorus:
Heave away you ruler kings –
Heave away, haul away,
Heave away, you'll hear me sing,
Bound for South Australia.

There's one thing there that grieves my mind –
It's leaving Nancy Blair behind.

I'll tell you the truth and tell you no lie –
I'll love that girl till the day I die.

As I was walloping around Cape Horn –
I'd wished to God, I'd never been born.

And now I'm on a foreign strand –
With a bottle of whisky in my hand.

I'll drink one glass to the foreign shore –
And another to the girl that I adore.

Fare thee well, and fare thee well –
And sweet news to my girl I'll tell.

The verses are sung one line then the first line of the chorus, and the second line followed by the second line of the chorus.

MAP OF PLACE NAMES IN THE SONGS
Cowan Downs
Flinders R.
Yanko Cr.
Winton
QUEENSLAND
Cooper R.
Barcoo R.
Augathella
Burnett R.
Maranoa R.
Castlereagh R.
Tilbooroo
Moonie R.
Brisbane
Toowong
Moreton Bay
SOUTH AUSTRALIA
Barwon R.
Mungindi
Wingadee
One Tree
Darling R.
Bourke
Louth
Dunlop
Gunnedah
Breeza
Kempsey
Port Macquarie
NEW SOUTH WALES
Euabalong
Goobang Cr.
Trida
Roto
Forbes
Canowindra
Castle Hill
Willandra
Lachlan R.
Emu Plains
Circular Quay
Moulamein
Murrumbidgee R.
Sydney
Woolloomooloo
Adelaide
Murray R.
Narrandera
Goulburn
Darlinghurst
Jerilderie
Wagga
Gundagai
Botany Bay
VICTORIA
Mt Kosciusko
Fiery Creek
Bendigo
Glenrowan
Beechworth
Ballarat
Mansfield
Bungaree
Castlemaine
Wombat Hills
Coleraine
Melbourne
Geelong
Bairnsdale

THE BUSHWACKERS BAND

The seeds of The Bushwackers Band were sown in 1970-71 at La Trobe University in Melbourne, where members of the folk club found a common love of Australian bush music. From sessions at pubs – notably the South Morang, outside Melbourne, and the Polaris Inn, Carlton – the idea of a band grew. The music at these occasions was as it still is – aggressive, humorous and involving all spectators, inviting anyone to join the fun. In 1971 the three original members, Jan Wositzky, Dave Isom and Bert Kahanoff, were joined by Mick Slocum, accordionist from Canberra, and a band was born, named The Original Bushwackers and Bullockies Bush Band.

The members in these early years were students and the music was a part-time occupation until 1973 when they decided to abandon their academic studies and play with the band full time. The first venture was a self-organised tour of New Zealand in June and the recording of a single 'When the Rain Tumbles Down in July'. By then The Bushwackers, as they became known, were popular in the folk clubs, on campus and in the pubs which is where the early band gained its stage experience. The music was simple, aggressive, rough around the edges and lighthearted.

Travel broadened The Bushwackers' outlook and aspirations. The year 1974 saw the Band's first European tour and production of their first LP. The Band had been joined by Dobe Newton, lagerphonist extraordinaire, and its name had spread to all corners of Australia. The Band that played the British Isles and Europe in 1974/75 had gained much professional experience and further musical vision by contact with such groups as The Chieftains, The Dubliners, Fairport Convention and Steeleye Span.

Throughout its career, The Bushwackers Band has resolutely stuck to playing Australian music and to date the repertoire has been drawn exclusively from traditional country songs and tunes of Australia. Australian folk music is bush grown but of Celtic roots; to its basic repertoire the Band has added some Irish jigs and reels for local adaptations of traditional British Isles set dances.

Much of the very early repertoire is still played by the Band today, though over the years the arrangements and style have changed often.

The Bushwackers Band has now travelled all over Australia, visiting isolated communities in the outback of New South Wales, the Northern Territory, Western Australia and Queensland, as well as all of the major cities. The Band has toured overseas six times. They have played and sung Australian songs in Germany, France, Holland, Brittany, New Zealand, Indonesia and Hong Kong, as well as England, Scotland and Ireland.

The original band in 1971

The Band plays all the acoustic instruments, including bass guitar, electric guitar and electric piano. There are also favourite bush instruments that the Band employs, sounds that they have revived that were nearly lost.

Spoons   Household soup spoons, silver if possible.

Bones   Cows' ribs, when dry, are excellent percussion reminiscent of the Spanish castanet.

Lagerphone or *Murrumbidgee River Rattler*   An upright pole with two crosspieces upon which are screwed beer bottle tops. The noise is made by hitting the instrument on the floor, at the same time striking the middle section with a solid piece of wood.

Bodhran   This is a Celtic word for 'goatskin drum', an Irish instrument unique in sound and style of playing.

Harmonica and *Tin Whistle*   These were popular instruments in the bush as they were very portable.

Concertina   Also very portable; it must have been one of the main instruments in the bush.

Fiddle   The devil's instrument, a favourite at the bush dance.

Accordion   There was much squeezebox playing in this country, not only by the Irish but also by the Germans who arrived in the Gold Rush.

FURTHER READING

The Big Book of Australian Folk Song, Ron Edwards, Rigby, Adelaide, 1976.

The Penguin Australian Song Book, compiled by John Manifold, Penguin, Harmondsworth and Melbourne, 1964.

The Second Penguin Australian Song Book, compiled by Bill Scott, Penguin Books, Melbourne, 1980.

Complete Book of Australian Folk Lore, compiled by Bill Scott, Ure Smith, Sydney, 1976.

The Penguin Book of Australian Ballads, edited by Russel Ward, Penguin Books, Harmondsworth and Melbourne, 1964.

Australian Bush Ballads, edited by Douglas Stewart and Nancy Keesing, Angus and Robertson, Sydney, 1974.

Folk Songs of Australia, John Meredith and Hugh Anderson, Ure Smith, Sydney, 1968.

Great Australian Folk Songs, John Lahey, Hill of Content, Melbourne, 1965.

The Australian Legend, Russel Ward, Oxford University Press, Melbourne, 1966.

While the Billy Boils (short stories), Henry Lawson, Lloyd O'Neil, Melbourne, 1970.

Joe Wilson's Mates (short stories), Henry Lawson, Lloyd O'Neil, Melbourne, 1970.

In the Days When the World Was Wide (poetical works of Henry Lawson), Lloyd O'Neil, Melbourne, 1970.

Collected Verse of A. B. Paterson, Angus and Robertson, Sydney, 1966.

The Bushwackers Band Dance Book, Greenhouse Publications, Melbourne, 1980.

Old Bush Songs, edited by Douglas Stewart & Nancy Keesing, Angus & Robertson, Sydney, 1976.

The Queensland Centenary Pocket Songbook, Edwards & Shaw, Sydney.

A Treasury of Favourite Australian Songs, compiled by Therese Radic, Currey O'Neil, Melbourne, 1983.

Down There for Dancing, Greenhouse Publications, Melbourne, 1982.

DISCOGRAPHY

LONG PLAY RECORDINGS

The Shearer's Dream, Larrikin Records
And the Band Played Waltzing Matilda, Avenue Records
Murrumbidgee, Avenue Records
Bushfire, Avenue Records
The Bushwackers Dance Album, Avenue Records
Faces in the Street, Avenue Records
Beneath the Southern Cross, CBS Records
Down There for Dancing, CBS Records
Lively (Live), CBS Records
Celebration, CBS Records

alluvial: surface gold.

ante-up: poker.

artesian water: underground water obtained from deep drilling.

B-bows: hand shears; the sprung steel handle acted to open the blades and was shaped like a B.

bell: rung to signal the beginning and end of a shift. A sheep arriving on the bell had to be shorn, and was not a welcome sight for the tired shearer.

billabong: a pond; strictly a bend in a creek or river which has been cut off from the main watercourse by the build-up of silt and sand during flooding.

blackleg: see *scab.*

blowing: yarning, usually boastfully.

bluchers: type of shoe.

blue: spend quickly and spectacularly, as on a spree.

blue mouldy: bored to death.

board: the floor of the shearing shed.

bone: many drovers and ringers took jobs between drives boning meat, a low status job for a bushman.

brownie: a 'fancy' damper made with the addition of sugar and currants.

brumby: a wild bush horse.

classer: the man responsible for sorting the freshly shorn fleece into grades.

cobbler: the hardest sheep to shear and left till last, usually a 'wrinkled, tough old brute'.

cocky: a small farmer.

colonial experience man: a popular practice among well-to-do families in Victorian England was to send youngest sons out to the colonies for some experience. Often used as a punishment for youthful indiscretion.

coolibah: species of eucalyptus.

cradle: used to wash the ore on diggings near creeks and rivers. The rocking action washed out the dirt and left the gold in the bottom.

damper: crude bush bread made from flour, water and salt. The ability to produce light, edible damper is considered a bush art.

dander: temper, ire.

Darling Pea: a toxic plant from western New South Wales (a common bush colloquialism for madness).

deener: a shilling.

dewdrop: an axe.

duffer: a rustler.

funk: throw in the towel, give up.

gaffer: boss of the shearing shed.

gammon: a lie.

German band: many Germans came to Australia in the gold rushes of the 1850s. The German band, where the accordion predominated, was a popular and common sight in the bush.

gidgee: a low, scrubby plant.

gun: a top shearer.

gyp: the hurry-up; also to swindle or cheat.

jackass: a kookaburra.

jumbuck: a sheep.

kelpie: the definitive Australian working dog, a crossing of the dingo and the first border-collie from Scotland. The collie's name was Kelpie – a Scots word meaning ghost.

knocked-down: spent.

Kosciusko: Australia's highest mountain, named after a famous nobleman by prominent Polish-born scientist and explorer Paul Strzelecki.

leprosy: a reference to the 'diseased' state of a station employing 'scab' labour.

long blow: a long, sweeping shearing cut.

miner's right: licence for gold digging.

moke: a horse.

moleskins: tough working trousers.

nardoo: a flour substitute made from ground plant roots.

nark: to annoy.

nobbler: a measure of spirits.

pate: head.

peeler: a policeman, named after Sir Robert Peel who founded the London Police.

pinkie: champagne.

plonk: rough red wine.

prad: a horse.

praties: potatoes.

presser: the one who bales the classed wool in the press.

prig: to steal.

rang-tang block: a shearing cut to castrate rams.

rhino: money.

ringer: often used as a general term for stockmen, but in shearing parlance the man who shears the most sheep at a shed over a stipulated period of time- usually a season.

roll: of money.

rouseabout, rouser: a general handyman.

sawbees: a type of hand shear.

scab: someone who accepts a job which the trade union has declared 'black'.

screen: the table on which the shorn fleece is thrown to be cleaned and classed.

scrounge: to beg with cunning.

shanty: a rough bush tavern.

shout: to buy drinks for others.

silvertail: a flash, aristocratic type.

snaffle: (i) to 'acquire'; (ii) a bridle consisting of a straight bit and a single rein, used by drovers.

snagger: a clumsy shearer.

sou: a very small sum of money.

spieler: a 'flash' character, usually of dubious honesty.

squatter: a well-to-do landowner.

stones: used to sharpen shears.

stoppers: leather straps used to keep blade shears closed.

stick the peg: to apply oneself.

tar: used on shearing cuts.

toadskin: a five-pound note.

tomahawk: to leave ridge-and-furrow shear marks and cuts; the sign of an inexperienced shearer going too fast to increase his tally.

tongs: shears

tote: an illegal betting operation.

traps: the police.

tucker: food.

two-tooth: a year-old sheep; usual growth is two teeth a year.

Ward and Paine's: a brand of shears.

weaner: a recently weaned sheep.

wether: a castrated ram.

whipping side: the side of the sheep shorn last with long blows.

whips: lots of.

windlass: spoked device used to bring the ore up from mine shafts.

Wolseleys: a brand of shears.

yakka: work.

yoe: a ewe.

INDEX

SONG TITLES AND FIRST LINES

GUITAR CHORDS USED IN THIS BOOK

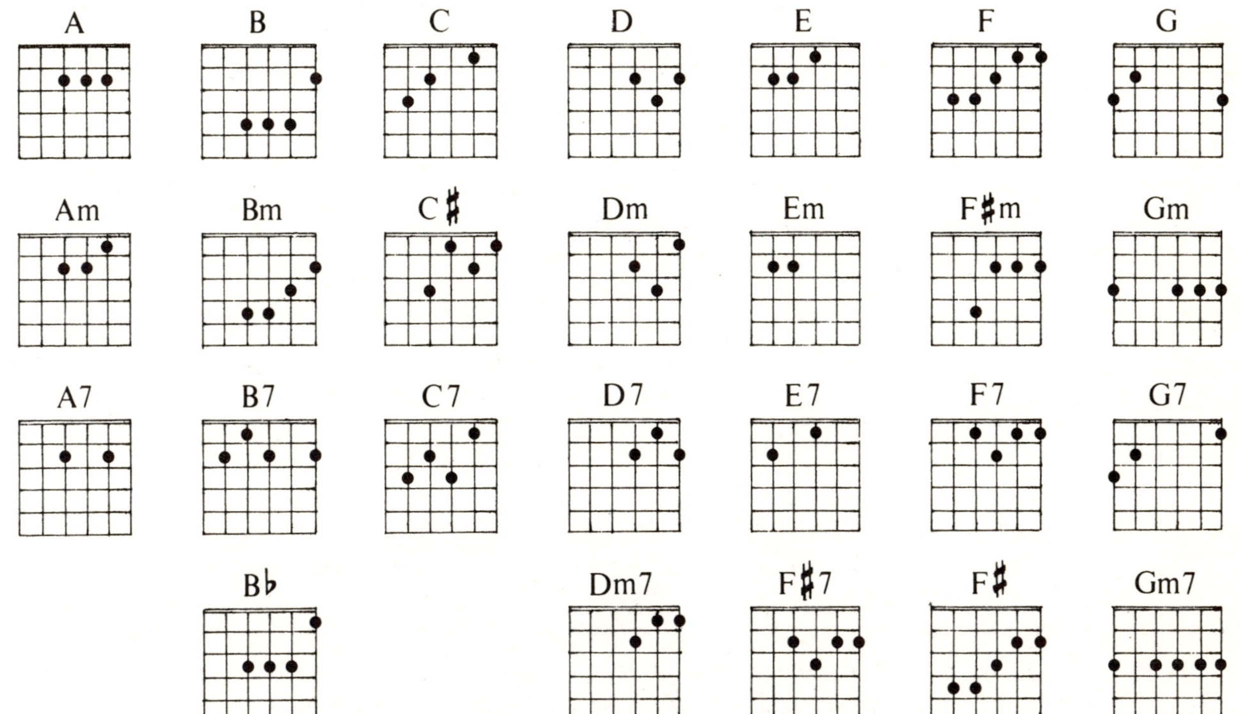